THE PSYCHOLOGY OF GARDENING

Why do so many people love gardening? What does your garden say about you? What is guerrilla gardening?

The Psychology of Gardening delves into the huge benefits that gardening can have on our health and emotional well-being, and how this could impact on the entire public health of a country. It also explores what our gardens can tell us about our personalities, how we can link gardening to mindfulness and restoration, and what motivates someone to become a professional gardener.

With gardening being an ever popular pastime, *The Psychology of Gardening* provides a fascinating insight into our relationships with our gardens.

Harriet Gross is Professor of Psychology at the University of Lincoln. She researches the psychological significance of gardens and gardening, was involved in creating a Gold Medal-winning design at the Chelsea Flower Show, and has appeared on national TV.

THE PSYCHOLOGY OF EVERYTHING

The Psychology of Everything is a series of books which debunk the myths and pseudo-science surrounding some of life's biggest questions.

The series explores the hidden psychological factors that drive us, from our sub-conscious desires and aversions, to the innate social instincts handed to us across the generations. Accessible, informative, and always intriguing, each book is written by an expert in the field, examining how research-based knowledge compares with popular wisdom, and illustrating the potential of psychology to enrich our understanding of humanity and modern life.

Applying a psychological lens to an array of topics and contemporary concerns – from sex to addiction to conspiracy theories – The Psychology of Everything will make you look at everything in a new way.

Titles in the series:

For further information about this series please visit
www.thepsychologyofeverything.co.uk

THE PSYCHOLOGY OF GARDENING

HARRIET GROSS

Routledge
Taylor & Francis Group

LONDON AND NEW YORK

First published 2018
by Routledge
2 Park Square, Milton Park, Abingdon, Oxon OX14 4RN

and by Routledge
711 Third Avenue, New York, NY 10017

Routledge is an imprint of the Taylor & Francis Group, an informa business

British Library Cataloguing-in-Publication Data
A catalogue record for this book is available from the British Library

Library of Congress Cataloging-in-Publication Data
A catalog record for this book has been requested

ISBN: 978-1-138-20787-5 (hbk)
ISBN: 978-1-138-20788-2 (pbk)
ISBN: 978-1-315-46085-7 (ebk)

Typeset in Joanna
by Apex CoVantage, LLC

Illustrations by Sarah Abbott

CONTENTS

FIGURES

FOREWORD

For centuries, gardens have been seen as places of restoration and renewal of mental and physical selves, as well as places of productive work and creativity. As I began work on this book, the UK health think tank The Kings Fund published 'Gardens and Health', a comprehensive report addressing the evidence for the value of gardens for health and well-being. The evidence is that the health benefits of gardening are important enough to warrant changes in policy and practice. The report provides a ringing endorsement for gardening.

This book is about gardening and psychology. Its roots lie in my own experience as a gardener and as an academic psychologist interested in what people make of their own everyday experiences and encounters. My questions are these: Why do some people choose to start gardening? And why do they carry on with it?

There is no 'psychology of gardening' as such, an area that specifically addresses gardening. Instead, to answer the 'why garden?' question it is necessary to identify what psychology there is that might help. Psychology is concerned with all aspects of human behaviour. Psychology investigates the amazing visual, auditory and mental processes of perception, attention, language, memory and reasoning implicated in everything we do when we engage with people and objects in the world. It is about identifying, establishing and explaining individual differences such as personality and ability, and how differences, together with gender, culture or age, affect underlying processes, identity and social relationships. Psychology is also interested in the contexts in which people do things, things they enjoy or dislike, and the impact of context on the fundamental processes that build skills, memories and relationships. The physical context for gardening is gardens (or their equivalent), and gardens are connected to nature and to all the other contexts of people's lives. There is a wealth of material on nature and psychology and on the other aspects of people's behaviour to explore in order to answer my questions.

The history, culture and practice of gardens and gardening has been explored by many distinguished writers from many disciplines. The wealth of gardening literature could be described as overwhelming. Coupled with an equally large field of psychology, and the many possible psychological theories available, the task of distilling the body of work into one book has been challenging. In keeping with the original plan for the book, the focus is on what psychology can contribute to understanding the gardening experience. I have had to make a choice about which bits to include. Inevitably, there is plenty of highly relevant and interesting material that I have had to leave out, that others might expect to see.

I look at what gardeners and others say about gardening, and I examine some of the psychological processes and areas that might be relevant. Additionally, I examine whether psychological theories offer insights into the reasons that gardening takes root.

Starting with an overview of what gardening is and who does it, Chapter 1 highlights how gardening is embedded in literature and history. The chapter briefly introduces the mechanics of research relevant to a psychology of gardening. Chapter 2 explores the gardening identity, through accounts given by individual gardeners for the significance of the garden as a place. The chapter harnesses psychological theories of identity and place attachment to help understand individual differences and the complexity of individuals' relationships with their gardens. Chapter 3 reviews different explanations for gardeners' descriptions of time in the garden. The chapter examines the components of Attention Restoration Theory and whether the concepts of flow and mindfulness provide alternative perspectives on the role of restoration and gardening. Chapter 4 brings together motivations, place identity and restoration through the theme of connection with nature, and considers what evolutionary theories can bring to understanding gardening as a way of managing with nature. The social and therapeutic use of gardening, based on the concepts of self-efficacy, restoration and connection to nature, is explored in Chapter 5, together with a consideration of the relative benefits of other activities in natural settings including garden visiting. The final chapter reflects on the opportunities and challenges gardeners face in the 21st century, concepts of the gardening career and expertise and the notion of gardening as occupation.

Harriet Gross, 2017

ACKNOWLEDGEMENTS

There are some people who deserve special thanks: Nicola Lane, Julie Taylor, Vicky Alfrey (née Roberts) and Hettie Roebuck, who directly shared my interest in the role of gardens in people's lives and who helped collect some of the material referred to in this book. Joe Fortescue, Harriette Marshall and Monty Don, and all the gardeners and non-gardeners who gave their time to talk to me about gardening. Rusi Jaspal and Susan Condor for joining me on the psychology of gardening journey. Lucy Kennedy at Routledge, for her interest in the topic and her editorial support.

Creating the 'Digital Capabilities' (Twitter) Garden for the 2013 RHS Chelsea Flower Show with Shaun Lawson, and Tom and Paul Harfleet, was one of the most exciting and challenging experiences of my working life. Huge thanks to them and to the whole project team for making the idea into an exhilarating reality: Richard Wright, Duncan Rowland, Chris Waltham, Peter Baldwin, Jamie Mahoney, Barbara Griffin and the Lincoln M.Arch students of 2012/2013. Thanks to the University of Lincoln for supporting the venture and to other staff at the University of Lincoln in 2013, especially Zoe Mead, Nicola Knaggs, Derek Cottrell, Norman Cherry, Mary Stuart and many more. In particular, thanks to Sara Owen for her unstinting encouragement and enthusiasm then and since.

Around the time I started to think about a book on psychology and gardening, I was part of a British Psychological Society working group set up to consider a possible garden for Chelsea. This introduced me to the garden designer Andrew Fisher Tomlin. Ten years later, because of Andrew, I got 'Digital Capabilities' off the ground, so thank you, Andrew. Sadly, the originator of that group, Stephen White, was not alive to see the garden in 2013, but he too deserves my thanks here.

My thanks to collaborators, colleagues and friends, many of whom are also gardeners: above all to Steve Brown, Sarah Burnard, Celia Dodd, Bridget Farrands, Caroline Gipps, Dave Middleton, Tom Ormerod, Ana Padilla, Helen Pattison, Jonathan Potter, Adrian Scott, Nigel Shadbolt and Jane Ussher.

Most importantly, thank you to my family. To my mother, Jane, and my grandparents Enid and Bruce, who planted the seeds of my interest in gardening; to my father, David, who loved to sit in the sun in the garden; and to my siblings, George, Oliver and Antonia. Last and most important of all, to Anthony, Daisy and Matilda, who have got on with their lives and put up with my assurances that I would 'be there in a minute' while I worked on in the garden as darkness fell, thank you.

1

STEPPING INTO THE GARDEN
The gardening context

Gardening is one of the most popular leisure activities. Twenty-seven million people in the UK report a personal interest or active engagement in gardening, and many millions of people visit gardens every year. When they are asked, gardeners can talk at length about doing their garden and the opportunity for being creative or growing their own food. If asked why they garden, they say it 'keeps me sane' or 'connects me to nature'.

People who garden at home or on their allotment are healthier and happier than those who do not. In 2004, the psychologist Aric Sigman suggested that regular gardening could cut health care costs, even claiming that gardening could be saving lives. Research regularly demonstrates that activities done outdoors (including exercise and gardening), the presence of plants or trees in outdoor and indoor public spaces, visits to urban parks and seeing natural views from a window can all lower stress hormone levels and improve adults' and children's mental health, well-being and productivity. There is now strong and growing evidence that nature is good for human physical and mental health, and that 'a regular dose of gardening can improve public health'. Given this ringing endorsement of the many potential benefits of gardening and nature, what does psychology have to contribute? The purpose of this book is to find out.

In its broadest sense, psychology is about understanding human behaviour and human relationships. Gardening is certainly a form of human behaviour, carried out in a particular place and involving a relationship with nature. Can it really save lives? What is the evidence for its positive effects? How does research explain the enduring attraction of gardens and gardening for some people? And where does that leave people who are no longer able to garden or are not interested in gardening? The following chapters examine the research and the theories that might help explain what is special about gardening and why it matters so much to the people who do it. First, this chapter briefly summarises some background information about gardens and gardening. It goes on to review how research is carried out to unearth more information about gardening and psychology.

DEFINING GARDENING

Dictionaries define a garden as an area, piece or plot of land, near to or adjoining a house, where plants, flowers, shrubs, trees, grass and vegetables may be grown or cultivated. A garden can also be a container, like a window box, planted with a variety of plants. In the United States, 'garden' refers typically to a vegetable garden and 'yard' (as in backyard) to a flower or ornamental garden. The definitions include gardens as parks or public recreation areas, or as 'ornamental grounds laid out for public enjoyment and recreation', such as botanical gardens. The verb 'to garden' means 'to lay out, cultivate, or tend' a garden or to 'cultivate as a garden'. Gardening is the 'job or activity of working in a garden, growing and taking care of the plants and keeping it attractive' and includes the concept of gardening 'as a pastime' or 'the work or art of a gardener'.

People garden not only at home if they can, but they also garden on allotments or similar plots, which are not necessarily next to a house. An allotment is a piece of ground let out for spare time cultivation under a public scheme. In the UK, allotment gardens are located on sites in towns, cities and in the country. They are owned and administered by local authorities who charge a minimal rent for

Figure 1.1 Definitions of 'garden', 'gardening' and 'allotment' from *Oxford*, *Cambridge*, *Merriam-Webster* and *Collins* dictionaries

the individual plots. These sites are usually run by a member association and often have outer boundary fencing although they vary in the way that individual plots are demarcated from one another, typically paths or hedges. Allotment gardens exist elsewhere, involving community or municipality ownership, making garden and growing facilities available to local residents without gardens or with limited economic resources. Allotments are strongly supported in Denmark, Sweden, Germany and the Netherlands. In Canada and the US, allotments are known as community gardens. In the UK, plots were originally intended for vegetable production, but ornamental gardening is allowed. Sheds or structures are permitted, but permanent residence is not allowed.

Gardening is defined as a range of activities related to a place, an activity and plants/nature, incorporating the concepts of work, care and land. Definitions encompass ideas of beauty and enjoyment. These ideas regularly appear in gardeners' conversations about their gardens and underpin evidence for and support the psychological meaning of gardening. Thus, gardening can be characterised as an activity that happens in a (private) bounded space or area, usually but not always near home. The human cultivation and tending of that space make a difference to it; with an edible or an aesthetic natural outcome. These two distinguishing features are explored further in Chapters 2 and 4.

WHO GARDENS?

Gardening is something that anyone can do, at any age and at any scale, as long as they have somewhere or something to garden. It is estimated that 87% of households in the UK have access to a domestic garden of some kind. Even without a home garden, there are balconies, roofs and window ledges for small or large containers, pots, window boxes and indoor plants in pots. Evidence from Australia suggests that homeowners there are incorporating more of their garden into space for the house, potentially restricting the plot for gardening at home.[1] Domestic gardens and allotments provide vital urban green spaces for wildlife and biodiversity, as well as spaces for personal and social activity. Community-owned and municipal allotments have had a resurgence; in some places the waiting lists for allotments are closed because demand is so high. There are also community garden projects and increasing sightings of opportunistic or 'guerrilla' gardening in unused spaces on pavements, around trees and in vacant or disused lots as well as roadside pop-up and pocket gardens, available to those without a garden (see Chapter 6).

Gardening is most commonly reported as a leisure activity by homeowners over the age of 35. In a 2010 UK survey, 62% of home-owners ages between 45 and 65 reported that they had gardened in the last 12 months. People under 35 are catching up fast, but only 16% of 16–24-year-olds admitted to gardening (*Social Trends* 41). In 2015 nearly three quarters of 65–74-year-olds were engaged in gardening in the UK, rather confirming the view that gardening is for old people. Certainly, gardening seems to be more common in older age groups. Also, 57% of the 27 million gardeners in the UK are women. It could be either that women are over-represented in older age groups because they live longer than men, or that gardening has special meaning for women (see Chapters 2 and 6).

Gardening is popular everywhere. In Japan, 32 million people (25% of the population) take part in daily gardening as a hobby; in the US in 2016, 118 million people (around 35% of the population) had gardened in the previous six months. Five million of these were new gardeners under 35 (the so-called millennials). In addition, there are many long-standing programmes and new initiatives taking place through schools and gardening organisations around the world. The goal is to get children (and other non-gardeners) engaged in gardening activities as a means of improving diet and environmental awareness and putting children in touch with nature.

GARDEN VISITING

Visitor numbers confirm the continuing popularity of garden visiting. For example, the Royal Botanic Gardens at Kew had 1.6 million visitors in 2015, and the Eden Project biodomes in Cornwall received one million visitors. In the same year, the Australian National Botanic Gardens at Canberra and Monet's Garden at Giverny in France each received around 500,000 visitors. People also attend national and local horticultural or garden shows and open their own gardens to the public. Under national and open garden schemes, around 4,000 private gardens across the UK (and Europe) are opened to the public every year (the proceeds of which go to charity), with visitor numbers well over half a million annually in the UK. The internationally renowned RHS Chelsea Flower Show, held in London in May, attracts approximately 157,000 paying visitors over its five days (a number limited by the site capacity), and millions see it on television (3.14 million in 2017). These formally recorded visits are only the tip of the iceberg, since they do not include regular everyday use of public parks in cities and towns, designed to provide 'green lungs' for urban spaces. Chapter 5 explores whether garden visiting has the same potentially beneficial qualities as gardening.

GARDEN HISTORY AND GARDEN MEANINGS

Most people who garden today do so in their own domestic garden or on their allotment, in the town or in the country. The principle of Garden Cities, proposed by Ebenezer Howard in the late 19th century, was to provide green spaces for private and public use and affordable housing for all citizens, with front and back gardens, on tree-lined roads (see also Chapters 5 and 6). His ideas led to the development of the first Garden City in the UK at Letchworth in Hertfordshire. They were subsequently carried through into other British planning developments like Hampstead Garden Suburb, and prefigured the rise of the suburbs, which arose during the expansion of towns and cities between and after the two world wars. The suburbs were seen as a refuge from city life, a peaceful place to return to and do the garden after work. The 'everyday Eden' that emerged in the process undoubtedly contributed to the iconic image of England as 'a nation of gardeners', and makes reference to an idyllic Arcadian past, where everything in the garden was lovely, if not for all at least for most. Gardening as a leisure pursuit for the many, rather than as a necessity or as a form of paid or unpaid labour, is relatively recent in the long history of gardens.

Garden history has described and delighted in the creation of both famous gardens that have changed the landscape and domestic gardens, specialist gardens and the human efforts devoted to the collection and development of plant species, and of course the various technical innovations (such as the lawnmower) to assist budding and established gardeners. Garden historians have also explored the value of gardens for personal and social pleasure, as well as changing fashions and techniques that influence how choices are made in and about gardens. In this history, the creation of gardens either as spaces for contemplation, beautification or food production represents the combination of nature and human effort that defines gardening. The meaning of gardens is also part of garden history; the idea of the Garden of Eden and Paradise as a garden has permeated literature, art and design. Gardens continue to symbolise, for example, refuge and safety, as well as represent social and cultural meanings of order and control over nature.

Gardens feature prominently in literature because 'they offer an abundant metaphoric range of images that help propel fictive, poetic and dramatic narratives'.[3] The concept of plot embedded in the garden metaphor represents not only a place but also the planning and execution of a political scheme or a dramatic narrative. In Shakespeare, garden similes can denote sinister goings-on. The 'unweeded garden that grows to seed . . . possessed by things rank and gross in nature merely' in *Hamlet* (Act 1, Scene 2), for example, refers to the depravity of the state of Denmark evidenced by the murder of Hamlet's father, and his mother's marriage to his uncle. Literature is filled with examples of the garden as a simile or as a metaphor, frequently for enclosure and privacy, for retreat, for hidden thoughts and activities and for representing natural (and sexual) instincts and human interventions into natural processes. Symbolising gardens as retreats has them as places of mystery and containment where magical things can happen. Frances Hodgson Burnett's *The Secret Garden* illustrates both the trope of the garden in literature and the concept of the healing power of gardens and gardening. Literary references to gardens abound, particularly as a proxy for keeping nature under control, including human attempts to overcome primitive urges. For example, in *Mansfield Park*, Jane Austen refers to the dangers associated with leaving the confines of the garden and straying into the wilderness beyond the garden boundary. The heroine, Mary Craw-ford, envies gardeners as 'the only people who can go where they like', able to transgress the boundaries between nature under control and the wilderness beyond; well-brought-up young women strayed beyond the gate at their peril.

The language and metaphors of gardening and cultivation are not limited to literature; they are part of everyday conversation. It doesn't take long to harvest a crop of English words and phrases that refer to some aspect of gardens, plants or gardening. Examples include being *rooted* to the spot, *cultivating* your potential, *sowing the seeds* of an idea, having *roses in your cheeks*, being *a shrinking violet* or *a late bloomer*, deciding to *branch out*, getting rid of the *dead wood*, avoiding being *led up the garden path* and *digging your heels in*. Online searches for 'growing' and 'cultivating' produce over one billion and 48 million hits, respectively. Clearly, gardens and gardening activities have taken root in people's daily lives.

WHO IS INTERESTED IN GARDENING?

Academic and professional interest in gardens, gardening and horti-culture has blossomed. Experts and practitioners in geography, sociol-ogy, health, sports sciences, occupational therapies, landscape design and architecture, as well as in the arts and literature, have dominated research on gardens and gardening. Despite the interest from other disciplines, gardening has received surprisingly little attention from psychology, apart from a study by a pioneer of the psychological benefits of gardening, Rachel Kaplan.[4] Psychology has tended to focus instead on the potential benefits of nature, where nature is a sepa-rate, go-to location away from home. And yet, 'gardens allow nature to enter the reality of daily life'.[5] If nature is considered beneficial and of interest to psychology, then the apparently mundane activity of gardening is a psychological experience too. Given that so many people do garden, and that it can be hard work, the question is: What does gardening do for them? The following chapters explore whether there is a 'psychology of gardening', what gardening offers people and how it contributes to well-being.

Before moving on to examine why people garden, the next section gives a brief overview of the ways that research has been carried out on gardening, and considers the methods and samples used in the research.

DIGGING UP GARDENING

Searching for garden research yields a long list of diverse projects. Projects explore leisure and gardening, gardening as a physical activity, gender and gardening, community and allotment gardening, gardening identities, environmental and ecological practices, the place of animals in gardens and cities, the meaning of gardens, gardens in literature and poetry, gardens as memorials, landscape and garden design, garden histories and garden visiting, to name but a few. Much of this research has something to do with psychology, because it concerns individuals and their relationship with nature. The area of psychology that directly addresses human–nature relationships is environmental psychology, and to a lesser extent the related field of ecopsychology.

Environmental psychology

Environmental psychology has a broad remit covering human–nature interaction and the investigation of the interaction between individuals and their natural and built environments. Kurt Lewin, whose work formed the basis for this area of psychology, believed strongly that behaviour is affected by the social (and physical) environment in which it happens, and that this environment should be taken into account in research. Environmental psychology started by looking at the built environment; now it has a greater interest in the biophysical environment. It examines how human behaviour and quality of life can be affected by good and poor environments as well as how human behaviour contributes to those environments. The remit includes ways to change behaviour that will reduce or reverse the human impact on the environment, in the interests of sustainability.

Ecopsychology has a similar concern with reducing the negative human impact on the natural world. It is especially keen to restore emotional bonds with the natural world, starting from a position that humans are disposed to be in touch with nature through a process of evolutionary experiences. The human–nature relationship is explored with respect to gardening in Chapters 3 and 4.

Researching gardening

There is no single psychological theory of gardening as such. Environmental psychology takes an interactive and collaborative approach, combining ideas from different areas, such as social psychology and health psychology, to understand how aspects of the individual and the environment affect behaviour or emotion. So research into the human–nature relationship, including gardening, draws on a range of theories and evidence. There are two inter-related strands of research on nature and on gardening. One strand involves the effects of nature (from wilderness to nearby nature), specifically, what makes natural environments beneficial and whether the effects are consistent (see Chapters 3 and 4). The other strand focuses on the gardener or the practice of gardening to discover what being a gardener means to individuals, by investigating personal experiences of nature, including gardening. This includes gardening as a therapeutic or healing activity in natural settings (see Chapters 2 and 5).

To examine these two strands, a variety of research tools are used to gather evidence. The tools include specialised measures of personality characteristics (traits, such as nature connectedness) or psychological health and well-being (such as mood or self-esteem). These are used to gauge how people are affected by natural settings, or whether personality affects environmental awareness, for example. Natural settings and environments usually mean rural settings or nature at a distance from home. Domestic gardens are considered a combination of natural and built environments because they are located close to houses or apartment buildings. Studies also use images of different natural or urban scenes, intended to represent views from a window, to test which environments people prefer. Images are also used to measure whether environments impact people's behaviour or affect their performance (e.g. on problem-solving tasks). Many studies ask people directly about their gardening experiences through surveys and questionnaires, or interviews with individuals or focus groups, and some research also includes analysis of textual material and images.

Although it might seem the obvious thing to do, using real natural settings rather than pictures for research has been limited because it is difficult to ensure that participants are experiencing the same things. Using images means that everyone taking part sees a similar set of features. Eye-tracking technologies now make it possible to gather details of where someone is looking in an image by recording fixation times and locations, but up to now this information has been difficult to gather in a real setting. With the increasing availability of virtual environment technologies (e.g. Oculus Rift), the possibilities for immersive experiences of natural settings are extended, giving a potentially more realistic and varied environmental context for studying the benefits of exposure to nature.

The following section summarises some key concepts examined in the later chapters and some of the practical ways that the two strands of research are carried out. The section concludes with a brief discussion of whether it matters who gets included in research on gardening and nature.

Key concepts in research on natural environments

Gardens have always been considered restorative. In environmental psychology, 'restoration' refers to the positive effect of an environment on individual behaviour or performance, and to the features of the environment that make it 'restorative', that is suited to recovery or restoration (see Chapter 3). Some research on restoration seeks to establish whether natural environments are more effective at restoring mood, stress or performance than built ones. To do this, people in a controlled setting (experiment) are exposed to a challenging experience such as watching a scary movie or doing a demanding task to induce a level of stress. People are then exposed to rural or urban environment scenes to determine whether one is better at reducing the person's level of stress. The studies can involve comparison with people who receive the stress-inducing task but do not see the scenes. The value of controlled studies like these is that researchers can be sure that the outcome is due to the rural or urban scenes presented, rather than other factors.

The other aspect of restoration concerns what makes natural environments restorative. Research investigating 'restorativeness' asks people to look at photographs of contrasting natural and built environments, and say how suitable they would be for restoration or how much they like them. The photographs can be of positive (e.g. attractive) and negative (e.g. dirty) urban and rural scenes. For this, environmental psychologists have developed dedicated measures of perceived restorativeness and restoration outcomes, so that findings from different studies can be more easily compared with each other.[6] Other studies ask people to imagine a favourite place and then rate it for how suitable it would be for restoration. Natural settings of open grassy landscapes with trees and shrubs are frequently preferred over more dramatic or forested landscapes and pleasant or unpleasant urban scenes. Preferred environments are likely to be regarded as more restorative. Favourite and restorative places are discussed in Chapters 2 and 5.

How people perceive and behave towards nature may depend on their connectedness with it[7]; that is, how connected or related they feel to the non-human natural environment. This connection may be part of their Environmental Identity.[8] Psychologists have developed specialised measures (such as the Connectedness to Nature Scale) to test whether greater interest in contact with nature might be an individual characteristic or trait that also determines behaviour in relation to nature. Thus, a person who agrees strongly with a statement such as 'I think of myself as part of nature, not separate from it' might be more likely to recycle garden waste or harvest rainwater and so on.[9] The concept of nature relatedness has emotional and cognitive or intellectual elements; people may feel strongly that they are part of nature and want to conserve it and also seek out and evaluate evidence that supports sustainable behaviour. The measures allow researchers to compare different people and to investigate relationships between nature relatedness and emotional states. It is possible that such measures would be useful to find out which people would benefit most from contact with nature, or gardening.

Individuals and the gardening experience

Research on individuals and their experience is the most varied. It explores what being a gardener and creating a garden means to people, investigates how gardening relates to identity and considers the relevance of gender. Such research often uses personal accounts and stories. Interviews with individual gardeners provide a rich source of information about people's gardening experience, and the meanings they attach to it. Some studies use surveys and questionnaires to gather information from larger numbers of people, which can include measures of health, psychological well-being and connectedness to nature, to help identify whether different psychological factors explain people's interest in gardening.[10] Work on gardening and meaning has used magazine material or historic images and documents, and the sociologist Mark Bhatti has made use of personal written accounts of gardens and gardening written material to explore the meaning and importance of gardens and gardening for people in Britain in the late 20th and early 21st centuries.[11]

Bhatti used a unique source of written material, the Mass Observation Archive housed at the University of Sussex.[12] The Archive contains material covering the period 1937–1955, and the original database has been regularly updated since through Directives requesting contributions on particular topics from panel members. In 1998, a Directive on Gardens and Gardening was sent out, asking panel members to write in about their own gardens, about sources of gardening knowledge, and about gardening and the environment. It resulted in 250 written responses and 350 photographs. The You and Gardens Directive (2007) generated 160 responses to questions about people's ideal gardens, gardens on TV and radio, environmental issues and whether they had special places in their gardens. In addition, 387 responses generated by a 1993 Directive on Pleasure and Enjoyment included references to nature and to the garden. Twice as many women responded to the Directives as men. Bhatti points out that the Directive respondents were writing for an (unseen) audience, which could affect what they wrote, and that the process of writing itself may generate thoughts that had not previously been present. Because researchers cannot follow up with writers or clarify content, the researcher/reader may be making partial interpretations which were not intended by the anonymous respondents.

Whatever the method, research on personal meanings of gardening so far gives rise to consistent themes which recur in studies of individual private gardeners, allotment gardeners and therapeutic gardening participants. The themes are ownership, identity and creativity; contact or connection with nature; escape or retreat; self-efficacy and being productive; stress reduction; and caring and social relationships or networks. The importance of being physically active also emerges for many of the gardeners studied. Some of these themes form the basis for the following chapters (see Chapters 2–6).

Who takes part in research?

Research frequently uses students as participants, especially research that investigates the restorative benefits of natural scenes or opportunities to spend time in natural settings. Studies of gardeners and gardening tend to involve older adults. Do these differences in the groups being studied matter? Probably not, since most people who garden are older. However, it is important to consider who actually takes part in research.

Access to participants is always a factor for researchers, and this relates to gardeners as much as to students. Allotment gardeners are relatively easy to access compared with private home gardeners, but there may be differences between private and allotment gardeners and non-gardeners that could affect the outcomes of the research. Some studies find no demographic differences between gardeners

and non-gardeners, whereas others found their allotment gardeners were slightly physically fitter and weighed less than their non-
gardening control group.

Gardening survey data also suggest that the gardening population
does not always represent the population at large. For example, gardeners taking part in UK studies typically include larger numbers of older
people and of women, most of whom are householders, than the general
population. Austrian and Japanese studies seem to include more men
than UK or US studies. Volunteers taking part in gardening studies are
more likely to be female, older, white, middle class, healthier and better
educated than those who do not volunteer. People less willing to volunteer are therefore excluded from studies, and less accessible to researchers, so researchers have to be imaginative to involve a greater range of
participants. On the other hand, therapeutic and community gardening
schemes are designed to encourage more marginalised groups to take
part, which means that these individuals will potentially have a voice
(see Chapter 5). So there may be differences between groups of gardeners, and between gardeners and other groups. The differences may
depend on age, gender, method of recruitment or the measures used to
compare them. Such differences may influence the outcomes of research.

By contrast, projects on restoration and on the human–nature relationship that underpin some of the psychology of gardening, have
mostly been carried out with samples of university students. One
reason for using students is that they are easily available to researchers and they may have experience of activities in nature away from
home. It is assumed that students are psychologically similar to each
other and the general population. However, university students are
likely to be more highly educated than a truly representative sample,
which may make them different from the rest of their age cohort,
at least. In addition, a study of 8,500 students at 30 US universities
suggests that the personality profile of students could vary depending
on the type of university they attend.[13] This casts some doubt on their
uniformity as a group.

Student-age adults (typically 18–25-year-olds) are currently the
least likely age group to garden, so their absence from gardening

research may not be a problem. However, their missing contributions could perpetuate a sense that gardening is not meaningful for young people. Younger adults do have some experience of gardens, and activities in gardens, and they may have different perspectives on gardening, which would be of interest to researchers. These issues of participation are by no means exclusive to gardening research, but may influence thinking about gardening and what it means to different people.

WHERE NOW?

Gardening is popular: it reaches beyond the physical garden space to appear in literature and art. There is some evidence that, like nature, it may be good for people, and there are a number of ways to find out more about this and gardening as a potentially life-saving activity. Critically, however, gardening is not just about nature; it is about people and their gardens, and this is where we begin.

2

'IT'S MY LITTLE BIT OF PARADISE'
What your garden says about you

Once upon a time, a Sunday newspaper ran an 'experiment' for a feature called 'What your garden says about you' and asked for my help. The experiment required me to inspect photographs of five gardens, work out what kind of person owned the garden and describe them. The final article would reveal whether my descriptions were right. The gardens were all very different, and no information was given about the owners. By chance alone, it would be possible to pick features from each garden and identify something that matched an aspect of the owner's identity or personality, so it was quite challenging. The published newspaper article revealed that two or three elements of each description submitted were close enough to make it seem a reasonable match. And one description was completely right – the garden owners' gender; four out of five were owned by women.

This light-hearted experiment assumed that gardens reflect their owners. Gardens are places for individual creativity and personal expression. People take considerable trouble to personalise their homes, so it would be surprising if individual experience or preferences, or indeed gender, did not affect the way their garden looks. This chapter examines the psychological value of gardening as a process of personalisation. Using research on gardeners' experiences, the chapter explores how personality or identity might relate to people's engagement with gardening. The final section assesses how gardening and the idea of place attachment are linked.

OWNERSHIP AND IDENTITY: 'DOING MY GARDEN FOR ME'

Interviews with gardeners and allotment holders testify to the personal creative activity that goes into producing a garden.[1] Gardeners' personal preferences are achieved through plant choices, planting styles and layout of the plot as well as structures and objects in the garden. In their gardens, people can express their commitment to sustainability (their environmental identity) through what they grow or what they do there. People have fond memories of their childhood gardens, and some have even had an idea of what they wanted their own garden to be like since they were children.

People emphasise their plot's uniqueness or its personality and are pleased to claim their heritage, relationships and experiences through their gardens: 'My garden is the result of many influences: my foster parents and my foster sister, my slave ancestry, and my travels . . . when I filmed abroad I brought back so many plants, in my mind at least' (Wesley Kerr, 19/9/15).[2] Similarly, immigrants to New Zealand from China said that bringing things from their country of origin into their gardens meant they were able to resolve some of the difficulties they faced being in a strange place. Doing this helped them to feel 'at home' in their new location.[3] In a sense, their gardens gave them access to their own past in the present, so that they could see a future. In the process of making them more familiar, gardens come to hold meanings of place, identity and relationships.

Gardeners can be very clear about what they want, to make their gardens personally meaningful, regardless of the effort involved. One person interviewed about their garden had such a passion for roses that his garden contained over 150 rose bushes. Somebody else had removed much of the planting and chopped down 'out of control' trees in her small garden, because it had been too 'granny-fied'.[4] Allotment holders construct their allotment spaces in ways which clearly reflect personal, local and national ideals. For example, some people grow vegetables not easily available in local shops. Iris said of her allotment: 'Just doing it up how I like it, it just adds that extra bit of individuality to it. I like that. It feels good'. Iris's comment exemplifies the emotional and sensory aspects of gardening; personalisation is not just about the appearance of her allotment, but also about how it *feels* to her.

Making a garden that feels good seems to involve starting from scratch. People talk about starting from scratch, or wishing they could start with a clean slate, in their home garden or on their allotment. Home gardeners mention the layout or planting that needs changing. Allotment holders emphasise how poor the plot was when they took it over and give detailed descriptions of their effort needed to clear it, especially if it had lain unused for a while. Clearance can mean several things: clearing unwanted nature, clearing away the previous inhabitant and clearing space to express their own identity, to establish their own personal style and to make the garden a place that feels right for them. Creating and cultivating a garden is clearly a psychological undertaking that goes beyond the horticultural and the physical. People's thoughts, feelings and behaviours are grounded in bodily interaction with the environment. Wanting the garden to feel right emphasises that gardening is not just a physical activity but also an embodied process.

Whatever individual garden style gardeners aspire to, garden experts distinguish between different forms and styles of garden related to the historic time, to the designer and to the location. These can be divided into formal and informal styles. Formal gardens, for example, are distinguished by their straight lines or geometric shapes, repeated plantings and a neat and manicured look; plants are kept within bounds with a strong degree of human management. Informal gardens have a looser feel. They may range in style from relatively minimalist, with limited specimen planting, to a more natural appearance, giving the impression of nature kept in check, to a more flowing or overgrown style intended to be closer to nature in the wild. This can be achieved by planting native species only or varieties that need little maintenance. In general terms, garden styles can be described as 'manicured', 'romantic' or 'wild'.

Figure 2.1 An example of a manicured style of ornamental home garden, display-
ing regular planting and symmetry

A gardening personality?

Environmental psychologists have suggested that the differences in
garden styles might reflect different psychological needs. They have
compared garden styles and aspects of personality, in particular,
people's need for structure (known as Personal Need for Structure
or PNS).[5] Greater need for structure is associated with a dislike of
ambiguity and an ability to be decisive. In an online survey, images
of romantic style gardens were considered equally attractive by people with higher and lower need for structure. However, adults with
a higher need for structure rated pictures of manicured gardens as
more attractive than wild gardens. Women generally rated all three
garden types as more attractive than men did.

The researchers then looked at the styles of the real gardens that
people actually gardened – rather than just using photos of unfa-
miliar gardens – to see whether there was any relationship between

gardeners' own garden style and their need for structure. They asked 123 Dutch allotment gardeners whether they would describe their own garden as manicured, romantic or wild, and they also measured these gardeners' need for structure. The gardeners with a greater need for structure (higher PNS score) were more likely to classify their own garden as manicured and less likely to classify it as wild. Men in the study were nearly three times as likely to have a manicured style allotment garden than a wild one. The men's preference for manicured gardens mirrors earlier findings that showed older men in Sheffield were more likely to appreciate neatness and less likely to enjoy the opportunity to be creative in the garden.[6]

It is tempting to say that people who have tidy gardens also have tidy desks, or that they are less likely to be creative than people with more informal, romantic or wild gardens, but this does not necessarily follow. The need for structure is more about decisiveness and certainty rather than being tidy in itself, so it might be more about planning and achieving an idea for the garden. Designing a manicured garden is inevitably a creative process. More importantly for the psychology of gardening, the study shows that the garden style people prefer is not simply a matter of personal taste, but motivated by important psychological needs. Possible implications are that some of the benefits of gardening could be reduced if the style of garden someone has at home or on the allotment deviates from their own preferred level of structure. It might also explain why the 'granny-fied' look had to go. The need for structure may explain gardeners' desire to 'start from scratch' or at least to make changes to their garden or allotment. Being a 'slash-and-burn' gardener, keen to keep nature under control and start afresh each year rather than letting nature take its course, could result from a strong need for structure.

Achieving a garden that feels good is partly about matching garden style to psychological needs. But this does not exclude aesthetic tastes, personal experience or potential individual differences, such as gender, age or other personality traits such as connectedness to nature. The need for structure could also explain the challenges for different owners of the same garden, expressed by Holly's reflection on her parents: 'Mum and Dad were very different gardeners. Dad liked his bedding plants and Mum liked to let things grow. Dad liked to plant things out every year and Mum liked her Christmas roses and things. It used to annoy Dad, he always used to call it Mum's rockery and Mum's buddleia'. Finally, the different needs for structure might contribute to disputes over boundaries or maintenance of shared space. It could explain why gardening in more public spaces, such as allotments or community gardens, can lead to tensions. For instance, the psychological fit between the person, the place and the gardening experience might be disrupted if people whose plots are next door to each other have very different needs for structure.

Identity refers to the subjective concept of oneself as a person including personality, beliefs and behaviours. Personality refers to underlying fundamental traits or factors that determine the way individuals approach the world. Psychologists refer to these fundamental traits as global dimensions of personality, sometimes known as the 'Big 5' personality traits. The Big 5 are Openness to Experience, Conscientiousness, Extroversion, Agreeableness and Neuroticism. Everyone has some of all five traits. Personality traits are a matter of degree. For example, two people can be extroverts, but one can be more extroverted than the other. Need for structure is likely to be a feature of the Conscientiousness dimension, which includes orderliness.

Need for structure is linked to preferred garden style, and connectedness to nature is associated with some gardening practices, such as organic gardening. Therefore, a garden could represent at least some aspects of the gardener's personality. Feeling close to nature (or nature relatedness, see Chapter 1) is also linked to the global personality dimensions of openness to experience and agreeableness. Features of these dimensions include altruism and concern for others and appreciation of art and beauty, which would incorporate concern for the environment and appreciation of the beauty of nature. People who are more open and agreeable are more sensitive to others' feelings or values and are willing to try new things. The features are also evident in gardening, which involves being concerned about plants and their needs and being creative and alert to the beauty of nature. So there is some indirect evidence that people who are more agreeable or more open to experience might be more motivated to garden. Some of those with tidier gardens might also be more conscientious. There is limited evidence for any relationship between gardening and other global personality dimensions of Extroversion and Neuroticism.

One study of personality characteristics and physical activity hints that extroversion has a role in determining choice of exercise, including gardening. Gardening was identified as a lower level physical activity in terms of energy expenditure, compared with sports and was associated with lower extroversion.[7] Lower extroversion scores indicate someone who has a positive outlook but who relies more on their own company to regulate their mood than on other people; this characteristic may be why gardening suits some people. One explanation for lower extroversion scores could be the age profile of gardeners, because it seems that personality traits change slightly across the lifespan: extroversion and openness reduce as people age and agreeableness increases.[8] However, the potential value of identifying relationships between personality and gardening for understanding motivations to garden is low, apart from suggesting that some types of people might be willing to persist with gardening as a hobby or be more creative.

What about identity?

In psychological terms, the experience of gardening and gardeners is more about identity than personality. The best indicators of gardening practices, such as Environmental Identity, are based on identity theories. Identity refers to a sense of self and assumes a level of self-consciousness or awareness. Identity is an inclusive concept, incorporating individual, relational and group levels of representing the self as it is influenced by culture. Individual identity includes personality, beliefs and behaviours. Identity can be revealed through subjective psychological experience. One particular theory, Identity Process Theory (IPT), offers a useful approach to thinking about the development of individual gardening identity.[9]

IPT is concerned with the total identity of the person and the way that the person seeks to construct and maintain that identity, which can at times be under threat, for example through positive and negative life events such as parenthood or illness. Total identity comes from social, interpersonal and individual aspects of a person's experience, and the development of identity structures is a lifetime process. Specifically, IPT proposes that identity construction is regulated by two universal processes. These are assimilation-accommodation, whereby new information is absorbed into the identity structure – coming to see oneself as a gardener – and the adjustment that takes place to become part of that structure, for example seeing oneself as a gardener and therefore in touch with nature. The other process is evaluation, which confers meaning and value on identity, for example seeing identity as a gardener as a positive aspect of the self.

The two processes function to create four identity principles, or desirable end states for identity: continuity, distinctiveness, self-efficacy and self-esteem. The four principles fit well with what gardeners say about their experience. So personalising the garden, making it idiosyncratic, enables distinctiveness, a sense of individuality. In doing so, gardening supports the gardener's sense of personal and social worth, their self-esteem. Gardening also provides an opportunity to boost their self-efficacy, their own feelings of competence and control. The pride and accomplishment achieved from cultivation and food production mentioned in many surveys of gardeners are indicators of the identity principles of self-efficacy and self-esteem. The principle of continuity refers to continuity of the self across time and situation and will be discussed further in the section 'Place and home'.

Another theory, Social Identity Theory (SIT),[10] proposes that a person's sense of who they are depends on the groups they belong to and which they feel aligned to, some of which are chosen (such as job, hobby or role) and some of which are given (such as gender or ethnicity). Groups define the characteristics of membership, in terms of behaviour and beliefs. SIT is relevant because the actions described by gardeners in the process of creating and maintaining their plot are a way of self-categorising as a gardener. Their actions confirm their membership of the gardener group, for example whether they are keen or weekend gardeners. Group membership also confers meaning and value on identity as a gardener. The extent to which individuals identify with a particular group, for example allotment gardeners, can affect how rewarding or energising they find the activity. The creation of the garden as a place, through gardening and personalisation, is both a reflection of someone's overall identity at a point in time and of the forging of their identity as a gardener.

Becoming a gardener

The idea of having 'greenfingers' or a 'green thumb' (US) is that some people have a natural (innate) ability for growing plants successfully. People may not realise they have greenfingers until they begin gardening. For some, it starts early; for example, as a small child watching acorns grow into seedlings, and knowing then that gardening is for them. Other people reminisce about being introduced to gardening by family members, grandparents or parents who gave them a space to plant seeds or jobs to do on the allotment, although garden chores are not quite the same as creative gardening or tending plants:

> For ten years I did a forced apprenticeship of drudgery . . . I never did anything interesting in the garden, I did everything from weeding to mowing so I knew how to do quite a lot but I didn't know any of the interesting bits . . . it's the exact opposite of how to get children interested.
>
> (Monty Don, garden writer and broadcaster, personal communication)

People come to gardening as a leisure activity, or as a second career, for a variety of reasons: wanting a hobby to occupy their time, wanting to do something physical and outdoors, wanting to be self-sufficient and produce their own food or because they finally have a garden. Like other leisure activities, gardening is pleasurable; it is a means of relaxation or escape from daily routines and a way of coping with stressful experiences (see Chapters 3 and 5). Serious leisure is the pursuit of a hobby activity that is 'so substantial, interesting and fulfilling that they [people] launch themselves on a career centered on acquiring and expressing a combination of its special skills, knowledge and experience'.[11] In becoming a serious gardener, individuals might progress from casual gardener to enthusiastic novice and then to expert. The more serious a gardener, the more likely they are to persevere in the face of adversity and to want to increase their skills. The capacity to undertake the tasks and processes of gardening contributes to the growing sense of identity and self-efficacy. The higher the level of engagement, the more satisfied with life people are. People who have been doing serious gardening for many years might call themselves 'enthusiasts' or 'keen gardeners', but not necessarily 'real gardeners'. By 'real gardener', they usually mean someone with formal training who is able to use Latin names for plants.

Gardeners who volunteer for research on gardening are probably keen or serious gardeners, because they have to identify themselves as gardeners in order to take part. Casual gardeners might not feel they qualify. In identifying as a gardener, and resisting the label of 'real gardener', people are making social comparisons: 'Well I'm a keen gardener I'm not just a weekend gardener'. As a non-gardener, all other gardeners are more expert, so by comparing themselves to non-gardeners, gardeners' self-esteem is high. As a gardener, the comparison can be with either non-gardeners or casual (weekend) gardeners, which will reinforce personal self-esteem, or with other serious (keen) gardeners, some of whom will always be more expert than they are (those real gardeners). In that case, even if they have been gardening for years, the comparison is more competitive; there is always something more to learn, and people's willingness to boast of their own skills may vary. Undoubtedly evaluation of other aspects of identity, for example gender, social status or education, will affect how people categorise themselves as gardeners.

A feature of serious leisure is strong identification with the activity to the extent that the hobby may hold greater appeal as an identifier (identity) than a person's paid work (see also Chapter 6). Gardeners certainly talk about gardening using work vocabulary: 'a 12 month of the year job'. They talk about setting up routines, keeping records and sourcing plants or other items for their gardens. Maintaining the garden is an ongoing project; whether hacking through weeds and battling with invasive species or growing a box hedge from cuttings, tasks can be a labour of love. But like all jobs, some parts are more rewarding than others. Sweeping up leaves can be one of the relentless cycle of jobs and a tedious chore; other gardeners are happy sweeping up leaves, even if they only sweep indoors under duress. 'I don't mind weeding, it's all those years of doing chores, and I'm in control now so if I want to stop I can . . . I don't mind weeding, I don't mind mowing, I don't mind raking leaves' (Monty Don, garden writer and broadcaster, personal communication). Contributors to the Mass Observation Archive gardening directives (see Chapter 1) reported with surprise that they actually enjoyed mowing the lawn because it was 'so satisfyingly restful'.[12] Of course, achieving the perfect lawn is an art in itself, often seen as a man's job requiring a high degree of dedication, exemplified by having to remove any weeds from the lawn every morning in order to keep it pristine.

The work of being a gardener is more than physical. People feel strongly about the sort of gardener they intend to be and what this requires of them. Joy, one of the Mass Observation Archive contributors, made it clear to her husband that she would do all the work needed and make all the decisions, so that it would be her garden, and that she was not going to compromise.[13] Her husband agreed to this, and Joy's desire to avoid compromise contrasts with Holly's parents described earlier, who managed by separating plants and locations within their garden. For Joy, being the gardener and doing the garden meant taking complete ownership. The sense of empowerment this represented for her suggests that the gardening identity may be particularly valuable for women, as a means of achieving self-esteem and self-efficacy. In the work of cultivating and tending a garden, women can be in control of their own domain (the garden or allotment), resist stereotypically female roles and assert themselves in other aspects of their lives. Although men are often handy for helping with the heavy lifting, gardens can offer a space where women are able to gain a sense of distinctiveness and develop new identities as gardeners, without compromise. This may partly explain women's greater participation in gardening, and their willingness to volunteer as research participants.

Gardening involves finding ways to express personal preferences and meet psychological needs. In the process, identity as a gardener is taking shape and individuals can represent their preferences and their gender through the style or structure of their garden and what is in it. Concept of place is integral to gardening; after all, it is impossible to garden without somewhere or something to garden. Place is not only a physical plot, container or location for plants; it is also a virtual place of meanings and identity. The next section looks at what the concepts of place attachment and place identity add to our understanding of gardening.

PLACE AND HOME: 'THIS IS WHERE I AM ME'

Becoming a gardener and doing the garden is a major commitment. It takes time and effort to create the vision and personalise the space. It also involves other people, real and virtual. Other people can provide physical strength and share the gardening tasks or decisions, and other people's presence can be represented through plants and objects. Family, friends and relationships mean social activities happen in the garden, and people often recall their childhood gardens as places for activity with friends or as inspiration for future gardens. These remembered gardens are also part of the person's present. Gardens or allotments can contain seeds or cuttings from other people's gardens, specimen plants found on a visit, or treasures bought for special occasions. Sometimes plants are used to memorialise personal events or special relationships, for example when children are born or people die. Gardens may provide a resting place for much-loved family pets.

Thus, the plot becomes a container for memories of people, events and relationships, allowing the past, present and future to intersect in one place; gardens have memories that are created and live on beyond the people who created them. More than this, the garden is a place of personal continuity (one of the IPT identity principles), providing a psychological thread or timeline between the gardener's past, present and future selves. This continuity across time is often expressed by gardeners who describe family gardens or previous gardening experiences. For them, gardening is an opportunity to rekindle past connections and manifest their relationship with gardens as a valued aspect of their identity. Identifying as a gardener involves creating the garden and doing the gardening of it. Moreover, the personalisation of the garden so that it feels right prompts a sense of belonging to the physical setting, which gives additional meaning to people's lives. Thus, gardening identity is closely associated with place identity, since place can provide information about distinctiveness and social identity (group membership). Place identity is 'best thought of as a pot-pourri of memories, conceptions, interpretations, ideas, and related feelings about specific physical settings as well as types of settings'.[14] When individuals draw similarities between themselves and the place, this 'pot-pourri' is part of their self-concept.

Place attachment and gardening identity

The garden is given meaning by individuals, who then become attached to the meaning as much as to the place itself. People often say that they cannot move house because of the garden. The dismay and resistance expressed when they have to consider leaving a garden or giving up an allotment make it clear that people do form strong attachments to their gardens: 'I would be devastated. It's part of me'. Being tied to a place – a home, a garden, a country – is associated with positive well-being, so leaving a garden may have an impact on self-esteem or self-efficacy, by disrupting the personal continuity provided by the garden.

Place attachment is described as a positive, dynamic bond between humans and a social/physical setting that provides psychological benefits.[15] Attachment to place can satisfy psychological needs, like

self-esteem and sense of belonging, and further implicates gardening as a means of becoming attached to a place. Factors that contribute to a sense of place and place attachment include place identity
and place dependence as well as nature bonding, social, family and
friend bonding related to place.[16] These factors all resonate strongly
with what gardeners say, and relate to the person, to psychological processes (emotion, cognition and behaviour) and to place, and
they are relevant to individuals and groups or communities. Places
serve important functions of survival and security, goal support and
temporal or personal continuity. These functions map onto the IPT
identity principles and the meanings that people give to their gardens
as places of attachment or identity.

For the person, connections to places that involve personal memories are likely to be stronger, and experience-in-place is important
in creating meaning. There may also be specific cultural, religious
or historical associations with a place, or places may be perceived
as spiritually significant because of experience in those places. The
emotion attached to place is usually positive; the evocation of positive
emotions is what makes a place attractive or restorative. However, significant places can also stir negative emotions. For gardeners who feel
optimistic about their garden, gardens are associated with positive
emotions of enjoyment or pride, but this may not always be true. For
example, gardens may provoke negative feelings for non-gardeners,
and as gardeners age, they may feel depressed by the tasks necessary
to maintain their garden (see Chapter 4).

Knowing and understanding how a place is organised, its familiarity and coherence, are also important in creating place attachment.
Like gardening, attachment is expressed through actions and behaviours that create the place as well as behaviours such as wanting to be
in or near a place, also called proximity-seeking. For home gardens,
proximity is a given, and for allotments, gardeners actively seek proximity. More commonly, proximity-seeking refers to returning to a
place regularly. Being securely attached to place does not require that
an individual is always physically close to it. In fact, the ability to leave
a place or object of attachment and return to it can strengthen the

person–place bond and is indicative of secure attachment. Gardeners are in regular contact with their gardens through their actions, and they leave and return to them on a daily or weekly basis (at least in the growing season), strengthening their attachment. However, because gardens are always changing, leaving them for too long risks things getting out of hand and creates uncertainty, which may challenge other psychological needs, such as the need for structure.

Being attached to a place is not necessarily about control over the space, since people may be attached to public places or spaces over which they have little or no control – people can become attached to their local coffee shop. Behaviour such as reconstruction, for example because of damage through natural disasters, also indicates place attachment on an individual or community scale. While there can be degrees of territoriality about place, which implies ownership and associated behaviours, such as personalisation or remaking of place, it is inevitable that social and cultural elements will be incorporated into the place, alongside the personal elements. As mentioned earlier in this chapter, Chinese immigrants to New Zealand wanted to incorporate familiar elements into their new gardens to help them create an attachment to a new place.

Place relates to both physical and social elements, with the emphasis on the social value of a place. Neighbourhood and community bonds formed through social interactions and relationships can overcome other less favourable aspects of an area, and place attachment may represent membership of different social groups, for example school friends, or parents at the school gate. The physical dimension of place is critical because it provides the location where psychological needs are met, for example nature or the garden is a location for having fun with friends. The places that people identify as meaningful extend well beyond the home space or plot to neighbourhood streets and buildings, natural settings nearby or at a distance, and for children include spaces not overseen by adults.

Lastly, research on place has tended to focus at the scale of neighbourhood and community rather than individual buildings or gardens. In reality, the kinds of places people feel attached to vary considerably in size. For example, attachment to a place of residence could range from attachment to a room, an apartment or house; a neighbourhood, city, country, region or even continent; or be a combination of different points in the scale. People may also be more attached to their home apartment than to a neighbourhood or district, even if their attachment to a particular city is strong. This work suggests that the scale of place that individuals favour may depend on their currently available space, in addition to their experience-in-place.

Garden as home

Heidegger says home is an expression of lived space, of human meaning and being in the world,[17] and Bachelard says that our home is our corner of the world.[18] Home can be seen as a source of identity and symbolic representation of the body, and these characterisations of home emphasise that it is clearly more than a state of being anchored in physical space. Home can develop through the practice of routines of care, building connections within the home space to people, events and actions within it. Research on the meaning of home has paid little attention to the garden, though conceptions of home are echoed in the lived experience of gardeners. Home contrasts inside with outside; home is seen as a source of security as well as personal and social identity. Outside is typically seen as separate from home, associated with work and parts of life that are not under personal control. The availability or possibility of outside at home is not often discussed; although the domestic garden may be part of home, it may not have or evoke the same associations. One of the valued advantages of home gardens is personal privacy. Of course, the emotional response to home may be very different depending on whether it is seen as a place of safety or as a place of harm.[19]

Attachment to gardens could be the same as attachment to home and all that entails. Alternatively, and most obviously for allotment gardeners, attachment to the garden is separate from the attachment to home, which could explain the dismay at having to relinquish a plot. There may be gender differences in attachment to gardens. The same elements of nurturance and physicality that underpin femaleness relate to spaces inside and outside the house. For women in particular, whether or not they have paid work outside the home, they take responsibility for most of the work in the house. They identify strongly with home but often have little control over its space on their own account. The garden may provide women with a 'room of their own', and thus for women their attachment may be to the garden quite separately from the house aspect of home. It is also possible that the opportunities in the garden for nurturance and physicality are appreciated by older people as a source of self-esteem and self-efficacy or as a way to maintain continuity of their identity, once paid work has finished or parental duties diminish.

CONCLUDING REMARKS: 'EVERYONE SAYS IT IS JUST LIKE YOU'

The theme of ownership and identity illustrates the psychological value of gardens and gardening. Gardens and allotments are intensely personal places, where people feel that they can be themselves. Gardens allow their owners to express aspects of their identities, and of their personalities, through gardening and the creation of place. Psychological theories provide insights into how gardening as a hobby offers social identity as a gardener and can offer the opportunity to achieve the processes necessary to construct and maintain individual identity. The identity principles of distinctiveness, self-efficacy, self-esteem and continuity can be accomplished through gardening. So although opportunities for personalisation may be different in private and allotment gardens, it is indeed entirely possible for gardens to say something about their owners.

The positive emotions that arise from the work (activity) of creating and doing the garden are also the processes of attachment to a place where people feel at home. Being in and doing the garden is an opportunity to be 'at home' outside, and crucially, to be engaged with nature, another of the core themes that arises from conversations with gardeners (see Chapter 4). One of the regular comments made by gardeners about doing the garden or being on their allotment is that they lose any sense of time. This loss of time is explored in the next chapter, which also explores the concept of psychological restoration as it relates to place.

3

'TIME STANDS STILL'
Restoration, flow and mindfulness

Places take their meanings from a complex interaction of the person, psychological processes and the place itself. Gardens are characterised as calm and tranquil places away from the pressures of daily life. The place and the activity offer the opportunity for gardeners to be themselves and to inhabit a world that they have created. Gardeners say that when they are in the world of their garden, they are not aware of time and that in fact time seems to stand still.

Psychology has several possible explanations for the phenomenon of time standing still in the garden, and some of these are reviewed in the first section of this chapter. Three key perspectives on the interaction between person and place will be explored: the influential Attention Restoration Theory, developed by Rachel and Stephen Kaplan,[1] which identifies how natural settings can restore attention depleted by other demands; flow, a mental state associated with happiness developed by Csikszentmihalyi;[2] and mindfulness,[3] a process to achieve inward focus in order to manage stress. To start with, however, the psychology of time perception sheds some light on different experiences of time.

TIME PERCEPTION: 'YOU GO UP THERE FOR AN HOUR AND NEXT THING YOU KNOW IT'S TEA TIME' (TOM & IVY)

Perception of time is always relative. When people are busy and there is more information to process, time feels longer. When people are bored, time seems to go very slowly. Working to meet a deadline, time seems to pass much more quickly than one would like, and time feels too short. Probably gardeners are not aware of time passing because they are absorbed in what they are doing. There are always chores to be done or plants which demand attention, and time is irrelevant. Gardeners generally see this as a positive aspect of gardening; families or partners may not see it quite the same way.

As well as being busy, the way time passes while gardening marks a transfer from objective clock time to subjective time or 'nature's time', whereby stopping and starting are determined by the activity or by darkness falling. Tasks can be continuous, like weeding, or episodic like mowing the grass or simply 'pottering'. Natural time includes daily times of sunrise and sunset, the time taken to grow from seed, as well as cyclical time of the seasons. In the garden, there is no externally imposed infrastructure that arranges people into rhythms of activity which are punctuated by events, such as meetings or meals, so people can 'switch off' from their routines. Switching off can be from clock time, from daily chores or stresses in other areas of life, and from cultural expectations of roles and identities. Similar experiences occur on holiday, or at other times when routines are changed; the more you do, the more time there seems to be. Perhaps it is not surprising that gardeners feel time passing differently.

Gardeners' perception is usually that time in the garden is shorter than it actually is; Tom and Ivy's planned hour simply slips away. Research on the psychology of time perception assesses people's ability to judge time passing according to the equivalence between perceived time and clock time, usually for short fixed periods of time up to a few minutes. Being able to judge time accurately depends on age; younger people are typically more accurate in judging the passing of time than older people, for whom time appears to go slightly faster;

that is, their judgement is less accurate. For example, if asked to count for 3 minutes, older people will say that 3 minutes has passed after 3 minutes 40 seconds, whereas younger people will judge the 3 minutes almost exactly. If every 3 minutes gained nearly another minute, it is easy to see how an hour on the allotment expanded.

No single region of the brain is responsible for time perception, which is spread between different brain areas. There is a link between the internal tracking of time and the level of dopamine, a brain transmitter. If dopamine receptors are activated by something new or exciting, the internal clock speeds up. The higher the level of dopamine, the more signals are being transmitted, the faster the internal tracking of time, giving a sense of time lengthening or standing still. However, dopamine levels change over the lifetime, reducing from early adulthood onwards and declining through old age. So it is possible that lower dopamine levels may explain why time seems shorter in the garden than it actually is, or that increases in dopamine, arising from the engagement in gardening, may account for time appearing to stand still. Time perception is affected by negative emotions like fear, because of increased arousal similar to a stress response (e.g. higher pulse rate and blood pressure), which speeds up the internal clock and leads to overestimation of time, so a brief distressing incident feels as if it lasts for ages. However, the perception of how long an unpleasant experience, that happened in the garden, had lasted could impact on someone's future interest in taking up gardening.

Emotion may also contribute to the feeling of time speeding up. Older people who say they are happy feel time passing quickly but those who feel sad, particularly sadness about their past, can feel time slowing down. Thus, the relationship with emotion is not straightforward.[4] Gardeners often report being happier than other groups, and older people in general have a tendency to focus on the positive. If that is the case, the sense that time has speeded up may reflect their mood. The feeling that time speeds up is also thought to be a factor of increasing familiarity with day-to-day experiences as people age, so that they need to give every day less attention and effort. This contrasts with children for whom the world is full of new experiences that require attention, and where school holidays seem to last forever.

It appears that several different mechanisms may impact on gardener's time perception in addition to the freedom from routine and the absorbing nature of the work. The phenomenon of time passing quickly or standing still, and the chance to switch off from clock time and on to nature's time makes gardening pleasurable. Psychologically, the ability to switch off may be as much determined by the environment as by the person, and has been related to the need for restoration following mental effort.

RESTORATION AND BEING IN A DIFFERENT WORLD

When people are asked to identify places that they would seek out to distance themselves from ordinary aspects of life, they frequently indicate a strong preference for natural settings. People tend to approach natural settings with positive expectations because of their own links with other physical or social experiences that have taken place there. These can be favourite places and places which match with identity (authenticity), arising from doing something that demonstrates their self-esteem. Natural scenes are also associated with improved alertness and performance, and boost well-being (see Chapter 4). Contact with or exposure to nature has an immediate effect on emotion via the parasympathetic nervous system (the 'rest and digest' system, which regulates and maintains the vital functions of the body like metabolic rate), leading to a sense of well-being and relaxation, and may explain why gardeners are happier than non-gardeners.

Stress Reduction Theory[5] concerns the effect of nature on the body and nervous system, and it suggests that humans are predisposed towards natural stimuli and find them relaxing. The capacity of natural settings to have this effect was taken up by Attention Restoration Theory, developed to establish 'what nature does, for whom and in what circumstances'.[6]

Attention Restoration Theory

Attention Restoration Theory (ART) has been one of the few psychological approaches to specifically identify gardens and gardening as part of the natural environment. The theory tries to account for the restorativeness of 'nearby nature' as much as nature at a distance, following a period of directed attention or mental fatigue. Nearby nature refers to parks, green spaces and street planting in built-up urban and suburban areas, and to gardens including window boxes and balconies, as well as to views of nature or gardens from windows. Directed or focused attention means making the effort to attend to something – the report to be written or the event to run – whereas involuntary attention requires no effort: something happens and you pay attention to it. Mental fatigue is the outcome of having to direct or focus attention on the task in hand and simultaneously avoid distractions. Mental (attentional) fatigue is not a negative state or a stress response (such as increased heart rate). When a person is mentally fatigued, they will leap enthusiastically into action when something new comes along. Physiologically, the 'fight or flight' stress response involves preparation for something potentially harmful or threatening by releasing stress hormones. Unlike mental fatigue, someone experiencing stress may struggle to rouse themselves to respond to anything new, however exciting it is, or they may become over-stimulated and unable to act.

Directing attention and avoiding distractions is increasingly challenging, or mentally fatiguing, in a world of constant connection through mobile phones or social media. One way to restore directed attention is physical rest through sleep, which permits consolidation of processing done during active periods, and dreaming, which is essential for mental health. But people need other ways to recover directed attention and free up thought processes during working hours or leisure time. These ways should make limited demand on directed attention and offer exposure to stimuli which are interesting in themselves. ART identified four key factors that environments need to be able to provide in order to restore attention and proposes that these are particularly associated with nearby nature. The four factors are *being away*, *extent*, *fascination* and *compatibility*. Each of these will be described in relation to gardens or gardening.

Being away means that a setting needs to allow psychological distance and a change of scene. The shift from one environment to another

frees up mental activity that would otherwise require directed attention. Paradoxically, nearby nature is not actually distant, but to be
restorative, the change of scene can be virtual as much as physical.
The important thing is the separation from the daily routine. This
change of scene is common to ideas of a retreat and implies an escape
from one thing to another. For most people who live in large met-
ropolitan and urban areas, natural settings fulfil the essence of being
away, but nearby nature can provide a change of scene. Certainly
many gardeners report the opportunity to switch off and enjoy the
surroundings when they are out in the garden, while they check the
seedlings or smell the sweet peas: 'I can switch off or I can think about
work . . . you do put things more into perspective'.

Extent means that the elements in the setting need to feel connected
for the person; that is, they need to be inter-related in a meaningful
way. Gardens and gardening provide physical and virtual connectedness to other parts of the gardener's life and to other people as well
as to nature. The elements also need to have scope, to be seen as part
of a larger whole. To achieve scope, the setting must attract sufficient
interest, something to explore that goes beyond the immediate perception of the environment and relates to the need to understand
and explore natural environments (see Chapter 4). Japanese gardens
are considered perfect examples of scope, because they offer more
to explore than it seems at first. Moreover, because gardens are a
miniature version of landscape, what a park can do by scale they can
provide through intensity. The garden can be a 'whole other world', so
it does have extent, whereas other green spaces can have extent by
dint of their design or their scale. Gardens afford both connectedness
and scope, because of their reach beyond the physical space of the
garden through family history and links to other places. Extent and
being away appear to refer to aspects of nature on a larger scale than
the domestic garden or allotment. However, seeing bees on lavender
can be as awe-inspiring as watching a waterfall and can transport the
observer way beyond the ground they are occupying, which contributes to the sense of time standing still. Feeling part of something
beyond the self is also the essence of environmental identity.

Fascination means what it says. It refers to the way that nearby nature or nature at a distance can attract attention and allow people to function without using directed attention as well as prevent them from becoming bored. Fascination can be soft or hard. Soft fascination comes from the aesthetic of the natural setting. The reason that natural environments and nature are seen as so fascinating and thus potentially restorative is that in addition to plants and animals, nature has such a variety of objects, forms and activities that can fascinate. Clouds, sunsets, scenery, ripples in still water or rustling leaves capture attention without making demands, encouraging reflection. The aesthetic is pleasing and uses little mental energy, and soft fascination allows sufficient mental space to explore other thoughts or issues that might be of concern. The potential for fascination to be restorative may differ according to a person's level of engagement or need. For example, people who work in forestry can find forest walks less restorative than people who do not have daily contact with trees, and they might find a coastal walk more fascinating.

The attraction of fascination is the opportunity to let the mind wander, achievable in nearby nature and in the garden. The combination of soft fascination with extent and seeing nearby nature as part of something larger can also contribute to restoration. In the development of ART, the evidence for fascination was the 'attention-holding power of the garden', which was considered one of the most beneficial aspects of gardens by the participants in the Kaplans' studies. Attention-holding power is hard fascination, the opportunity to be completely engaged in the setting, an intense engagement that leaves little room for reflection: 'I completely forget about anything else', and it might well account for time seeming to stand still in the garden.

Compatibility means that the new setting, the actions required of the person by that environment and an individual's inclinations must all be compatible with each other. There are a number of different ways for people to relate to the natural environment, which will determine what they are looking for as compatibility. People can be actively part of nature as walkers or wild swimmers; they can be passive observers like birdwatchers; as gardeners or beekeepers they can be cultivators or carers. They can also be hunters and anglers. If the objects in the chosen environment fascinate and provide the information needed for action in the setting, then compatibility can develop. It implies that different people will prefer some types of environments rather than others for compatibility, or that experience in a setting may predispose them to future compatibility. For gardeners, gardens provide compatibility, but for non-gardeners, gardens can still be restorative, through extent, soft fascination or being away. One reason that gardening may provide compatibility is that there is a sense of authenticity about it, the actions taken in the setting make a difference, something important for maintaining identity.

Gardens offer both soft and hard fascination, contributing to the experience of gardening as an 'attention-holding' activity. They permit compatibility, and they are places that permit being away and extent. In this sense, therefore, gardens and gardening are restorative. A survey of 566 adults in Austria who were asked to complete the Perceived Restorativeness Scale rated private gardens as restorative and indicated that enjoyment of the garden, satisfaction and connectedness with it contributed most to making the garden restorative.[7]

Recovery and reflection are separate aspects of restoration and, as the earlier descriptions suggest, the four environmental factors do not contribute equally to both of these aspects. For some people, being in the garden is about reflection, a time to escape from pressures of work and think of nothing. For others, the garden is identified as a place to undertake demanding activities such as exam revision or to think about work. For them, the location may be more about individual coping strategies rather than restoration itself.

Exposure to nearby nature does not have to be for long periods to have an impact. Micro-restorative experiences of nature have been found to be effective in sustaining attention or reducing stress, for example looking through a window at greenery,[8] or views of a green (planted) roof, for as little as 40 seconds.[9] Similarly, experiences of and in nature, such as hearing birdsong or walking through a green area, can have an energising 'instorative' effect on mood and energy, rather than a 'restorative' one, for people who are not stressed or mentally fatigued.[10] These incidental aspects of the natural setting are undoubtedly part of the attraction of gardening. Coming across them elsewhere can transport people to other places or times they encountered them, including to the garden or allotment. Simply being on the allotment, or looking into the garden from the house, might have an instorative or a restorative effect and contribute to how gardeners feel that their gardens allow them to switch off from time.

Although natural settings and nearby nature are often preferred, they are not the only kind of restorative environment. In fact, restoration may be found in many places, depending on time available, life stage and identity, and of course gardeners may do other activities that bring them into different environments where recovery or reflection can occur.

For children and adolescents, outdoor activity with friends may be more important for restoration than nearby nature alone. For young people and adults, restorative experiences were more likely to be described as exciting than relaxing (e.g. surfing or dancing), and for younger people, the longer the period available the more likely they would be to seek exciting experiences. They are also more interested in physically *being away* in order to distance themselves from daily aspects of life. Although people have fond memories of their childhood gardens, gardening is not always seen as an exciting leisure activity and may not represent sufficient psychological distance from home for younger people.

Places that people identify as restorative include leisure spaces which can provide the resources needed for engagement, relaxation and pleasure. People seek a range of experiences that can be home-based, going out in an urban environment or being in a natural environment. The restorative quality also relates to the presence or absence of social relationships in these activities and environments. For adults and older people, the longer the time available such as weekends or holidays, the more likely they are to choose relaxing environments and settings that offer fascination. Natural settings are not chosen more often than urban environments, although the more time and resources people have, the more likely they are to make visits to nature. Older people favour home-based activities more than the younger or adult groups do.[11] To reap the restorative benefits of an environment, people need to notice and appreciate places they are in, and this may require a complex chain of personal, psychological and place processes, discussed in relation to place attachment.

Research on identity introduces further individual variation that might affect the relative value of the four ART components. For example, people vary in how much they feel they are a 'city' or 'country' person. If this is the case, for a city person viewing urban scenes may be just as restorative as natural scenes are for a country person. To investigate this possibility, researchers manipulated the urban or rural identities of different groups of people in a short-term study. They gave the groups some information either about their local city, or about the surrounding country-side, and asked them to identify three things that people could do there. The groups were then given memory and motivation tasks and shown urban and natural images. For the group who had their rural identity highlighted, seeing natural environments was more motivating than urban environments. For the urban identity group, viewing urban environments was more motivating. This suggests that the capacity of environments to be restorative, par-ticularly the factor of compatibility, could be partly explained by individual identities as well as by experience in places, and people may be predisposed to prefer certain settings.[12]

In effect, more types of environments may be restorative, or dif-ferent types of environments may be restorative for different people. If individuals are exposed to an environment that reflects their own identity, the effect is positive. If the environments are not compatible with important aspects of a person's self-identity, they may appear distracting rather than restorative. The four ART factors specify what an environment needs to provide for someone to feel restored. Nearby nature is one major source of restoration, which can occur in a range of other natural and built settings. Individual identity, emotion and experience will be more or less relevant at different times.

Compatibility is about a good fit between individual inclinations and the qualities of the environment. It has many similarities with another psychological concept that addresses the phenomenon of time disappearing, flow, which also relates to individual skills. Kaplan and Kaplan, who developed ART, were adamant that the two are very different particularly because flow is about activity without reflection and is less concerned with the environment in which the action occurs. Nevertheless, reflection may not always be as important for gardeners and flow, focusing on process as much as outcome, can be a useful way to think about leisure gardening, in addition to the restorative value of horticultural activities and gardening.

FLOW: 'I JUST GET ENGROSSED IN IT AND IT TOOK OVER'

The concept of flow has been described as a highly focused mental state associated with happiness, a sense of being carried along by and completely absorbed in what you are doing. Time passes without being aware of it. It sounds like a description of gardening: 'I don't think of anything else at all, you just concentrate on what you're doing and it's a totally different world'.

The idea for flow stemmed from observing how painters created a painting and seeing that the painters were not motivated by the completed picture (something that a critic or gallery might want) but by the process of making the painting. Happiness came from the activity 'for its own sake', expressing who they were (identity) and what they were good at (self-efficacy). In psychological terms, the experience of flow for its own sake is a form of intrinsic reward. The description of painting resonates very strongly with the ideas on personal identity and being creative in the garden. In the original work, artists were so involved in the process of painting that they would miss out on eating or sleeping – the activity could almost be said to have taken them over – and time was immaterial, so they were psychologically distanced from other parts of their lives, like 'being away'. Not only is this familiar from gardening, but also it is reminiscent of the stereotype of the creative genius, working away in the studio or shed, forgetting to eat unless other people remind them to.

For flow to occur, an activity or occupation should have clear goals, which include that the expectations of the activity are attainable and are aligned with personal skills and abilities, and that the task is challenging but not so difficult that it would be abandoned. This sounds very like extent and compatibility, and like gardening. Other features that define flow also chime with what gardeners say about their experiences, not least an altered sense of time. The features include concentrating and focusing, working within a limited field of attention and getting stuck into things. In addition, the descriptions of flow refer to a loss of self-consciousness and a merging of action and awareness – a sense of control over the activity and a distorted sense of time. People describe losing the sense of self as an intermediary between stimulus and response. For example, a rock climber vividly describes being immersed in the rock, the moves, searching for handholds and being so involved he 'might lose the consciousness of his own identity and melt into the rock'.[13]

Flow has been used to explain people's enjoyment of activities, from playing the piano to walking but not gardening. As an individual, flow can occur at play, in sport and at work. It has been used in sports, business, education, music, computer games and many other areas, with the goal of improving performance. It is not clear exactly how people achieve flow, although people talk about 'getting into the zone'. This seems to mean that they start to engage in the actions, focus on the tasks in hand and ignore other interruptions. In doing so, they get drawn into the action and processes and can achieve flow. For example, by becoming completely absorbed in the process of learning, children and young people learn more. In addition, flow may be more often achieved away from the everyday routines of home or work, in a context of being away. It is one of the few psychological theories that has explicitly focused on enjoyment, which is why it is included here as a motivation for gardening. Flow is an outcome that is pleasurable in itself rather than restorative of other functions, although this may follow. The incorporation of happiness and enjoyment is a valuable addition to the idea of restoration, since enjoyment and excitement are less often mentioned, even if they are important motivators for doing something.

Restoration requires an interaction between place and person, garden and gardener, and feeling restored implies having previously been in some way depleted, or overloaded, which the environment can change. Achieving flow and doing the activity in which flow happens can be restorative incidental to the pleasure of the experience; gardening may be a particularly good example of this. Another concept similar to flow is mindfulness, a form of meditation. Thus, doing the garden permits *being away*, *extent*, *fascination* and *compatibility*, and may instigate flow and lead to a sense of being in a totally different world. The garden as a place can be a preferred setting for undertaking mindful activity or alternatively gardening activities may induce mindfulness.

MINDFULNESS

Mindfulness[14] is typically defined as a mental state, calmly acknowledging and accepting feelings, thoughts and bodily sensations. It is associated with positive emotion. The idea is to observe personal thoughts and feelings without judging them as either good or bad. It is not reliant on setting or context, but is dependent on the person and their capacity to attend to their experience moment by moment. The principle was initially considered as a therapeutic technique in clinical settings, where use of mindfulness leads to a decrease in stress for cancer patients. It has also been shown to help healthy people manage stress and anxiety and has come to be used as a tool for managing everyday stresses, akin to meditation. Flow and mindfulness have different effects on the pace of time; in flow, the experience reported is that time either has no meaning, or that it has speeded up – 'We started rehearsing at 7:30, and its already 9 o'clock' – whereas as a result of mindfulness, people feel a slowing down of time, in keeping with a lower level of arousal.

Mindfulness is effective in treating symptoms of stress and anxiety in healthy people and as a means of restoring emotional well-being.

It requires learning to self-regulate attention, in order to maintain attention on the immediate experience, and being aware of experiences in the present moment. It may also require self-monitoring to prevent ruminating on thoughts or feelings outside the present moment. Like meditation, it needs a period of training and practice to become proficient at managing distractions, for example, and maintaining attention.[15] So mindfulness is a form of directed attention, the result of which is a reduction of stress. This means that directed attention can be depleting or a restorative process in itself, a bit like the attention-grabbing aspect of gardens that Kaplan and Kaplan describe as fascination.

The principle of being in the moment and aware of what is happening has some similarities with flow, but attention is directed towards the self and not to an activity outside the self. Focusing in the moment could explain a sense of time slowing down and reducing arousal levels. The distinction is between the self acting on the world, whereby flow arises in the doing of an activity that absorbs all attention, and the inward focus onto the world acting on the self. Being aware of thoughts and feelings and how an individual senses the world around them can help people notice stress or anxieties in a calm way and garner the resources to manage them. Engagement with mindfulness may be linked to emotional intelligence[16] and also to well-being and nature connectedness.[17]

There is evidence that meditation can reduce anxiety, lower stress hormones and improve attention and cognition in human study participants. Meditative behaviour can impact on the brain, at least in the short term, which may increase its effectiveness. For instance, meditation increases brain activity associated with lowered anxiety (theta waves, measured using electrodes on the scalp). In addition, brain scans show that meditation training is associated with changes in the brain white matter, which relates to the efficiency of communication between different brain areas, and the changes continue even after meditating, albeit for a short time.[18] Something similar to mindfulness and meditation can be induced in mice, which show decreased anxiety behaviour following stimulation of a brain region (anterior cingulate cortex) that regulates activity in the amygdala, the structure that controls fearful responses. Mice that received stimulation with the equivalent of theta waves showed less anxiety than mice that did not or mice that had received a different form of brain stimulation.

The findings suggest that meditation, and thus potentially mindfulness, has an effect on the brain, which in turn accounts for the change in stress levels. In addition, there may be some short-term carryover of meditation training on the brain. These different forms of evidence confirm that there are mechanisms by which practices such as mindfulness may have their effect and endorse the use of psychological and behavioural strategies to reduce stress. Undertaking mindfulness activity in a garden setting can enhance its impact as a means of reducing stress. Given that one effect of contact with nature is lowered arousal, such mechanisms may also underpin behaviours like gardening.

CONCLUDING REMARKS: 'I CAN SPEND MORNING 'TIL NIGHT OUT THERE WITHOUT THINKING'

Three different psychological explanations have been considered in relation to the changing perception of time when gardening. All three highlight the idea that being fully occupied or absorbed in an activity adjusts the relationship with time in some way, either speeding it up (flow), slowing it down (mindfulness) or making it irrelevant (Attention Restoration Theory, ART). ART emphasises the need for a match between the person and features of the environment that enable *being away*, and *compatibility* as well as *extent* and *fascination*, absorbing the individual's attention in a way that removes the need to notice clock time, and allows reflection. Flow focuses on the complete absorption in the process of creation or performance that resists distraction to eat or sleep and speeds up time, making less reference to reflection. Mindfulness emphasises the need for reflection and to be aware of internal processes and experience in order to lower arousal and slow time down. In the garden, time can move from human time to natural time, shifting from constructed routines to task-driven or natural cycles. The garden also contains past and future time, selves and experiences, all of which are brought to bear on the activity and contribute to a perception of present time as relative. Combining the approaches foregrounds the significance of the place, and person in the place; each of them contributes something different to making gardening a rewarding and enjoyable experience, which relates to features of the setting, the way that the individual becomes embedded in it and the opportunity to engage in the process as much as to reflect.

Restoration in any setting, natural or built, is undoubtedly valuable, but natural settings may be more relaxing or energising (instorative) for people who are predisposed to benefit from them or at different points in people's lives. Features that make settings restorative overlap with those associated with attachment to place and include social relationships, enjoyment and relaxation. These may all require less directed attention because they are sufficiently fascinating or generate action that prompts absorption, leading to recovery of attention and lowering of stress. The type of activity may also be sufficiently arousing to increase dopamine release and speed up the internal time system, affecting perception of time. Age differences in time perception and preferred restorative qualities suggest that increased engagement with gardening by older people is because it becomes more meaningful over time, with more memories and associations, and replaces work routines and daily pressures. Older people also value social networks around allotment or community gardening. Restoration and restorativeness do not appear to be gender-related, although women's greater involvement in gardening might partly be explained by the opportunities for being away and compatibility, in their own space.

When they were considering restoration and the physical experience of engaging with nature in a natural setting, Kaplan and Kaplan found that as gardeners gained experience, the greatest satisfaction they derived from gardening was from the peacefulness and quiet of the setting and from nature fascination. This also meant getting completely wrapped up in the garden, seeing plants grow, working in the soil and working close to nature. The benefits of contact with nature are thought to stem from an innate human propensity to be close to nature, and this has informed theorising about nature connectedness and restoration. Whatever the perceived value of nature as a restorative setting, being a gardener and doing the garden involves a relationship between human and nature. As with any relationship, there are benefits and downsides. The next chapter explores the idea of an innate human relationship with nature, the form of the relationship and the need to collaborate with nature in the garden.

4

'IN TOUCH WITH NATURE'
The human–nature relationship

Being away in the totally different world of the garden is about contact with nature. Evolutionary theory proposes that humans have an instinctive (innate) tendency they are not consciously aware of that prompts them to respond positively to nature and living things in nearby and wild settings. According to the theory, therefore, the perceived value of nature may relate to innate human preferences. Gardens and allotments are a personalised version of nearby nature, reflecting their owner's identity, experience, need for structure, and their preferences, which may hark back to an evolutionary past. In the early 21st century, the role of nearby nature for basic physical survival is limited, although a desire to be self-sufficient in vegetables and fruit is more than simply a hobby. Urban greenery and private and public gardening projects are associated with better health and well-being for adults and children. Gardens and allotments as nearby nature are the epitome of the human–nature relationship on a domestic, or at least manageable, scale.

Prior to discussing gardening as a collaborative relationship with nature, together with some of the downsides of that relationship, this chapter explores elements of evolutionary theory, which refers to nature rather than to gardening. Two biological evolutionary theories, Biophilia and Prospect Refuge Theory, are concerned with nature and survival of the human species. Psychological approaches also attempt to explain people's tendency to respond positively to nature and their preferences for particular types of natural settings. These are based on processing of visual information, specifically fractals and perceptual fluency, whereas the concept of affordance looks at how the spatial environment can determine behaviour. Finally, the section considers whether landscape preferences are passed on through culture. The chapter continues by illustrating the relationship with nature through gardeners' own experiences and discusses the emotional benefits and challenges of working with nature.

EVOLUTIONARY RELATIONSHIPS WITH NATURE

Evolutionary theories which point to a human affiliation with nature raise the possibility that engagement with nature, like gardening, might be genetically coded. Connectedness to nature is a psychological trait which has been shown to determine environmentally sustainable behaviours, including how interested someone is in contact with nature or being outdoors. So it is possible that gardening serves an innate need for connection with nature, and probable that people who are more connected to nature are more likely to choose leisure activities that involve nature, such as gardening. The likelihood of a specific gene for gardening is low but the evidence seems to confirm that evolution has influenced human behaviours and preferences.

Biophilia Hypothesis

Attention Restoration Theory and Stress Reduction Theory referred to biophilia as an explanation for restoration (recovery) and instoration (mood energising). The Biophilia Hypothesis proposes an instinctive bond between humans and other living organisms, including plants and animals.[1] It says that humans have been predisposed to seek out and approach elements of nature or particular landscapes, typically grasslands, that would support their own survival by providing food and security. Survival was a process of trial and error, which involved both approach and avoidance. The opposite of biophilia is biophobia, a predisposition to avoid or to be afraid of certain natural settings or elements. Evidence for biophobia is stronger than for biophilia, presumably because failure to learn to avoid dangerous plants, animals or places reduced survival rates at a stroke. However, an adaptive response of liking or approaching particular settings may have facilitated something like physical recovery or mental restoration. In a harsh environment, this could have indirectly contributed to the maintenance of higher order cognitive functioning and improved learning.

The idea of an innate bond between humans and nature explains some positive effects of natural settings and gardens, as well as connectedness to nature and environmental behaviour. However, nature and natural settings are not always preferred (they can be actively disliked and avoided) and nature is not always restorative, so the process by which the innate preferences for natural settings emerged is not easily articulated.[2] Some preferred settings are as likely to be psychologically or culturally determined as by their survival value. For instance, familiar settings are chosen more often, people with higher need for structure prefer agrarian to wilderness landscapes, and environments are more likely to be motivating if they coincide with people's own identity (such as rural or urban identity; see Chapter 3).

Prospect Refuge Theory

Prospect Refuge Theory (PRT) was developed[3] to explain why people prefer certain types of landscapes and has been of particular interest to landscape designers. PRT also proposes that the modern preference for park-like landscapes is partly a genetic predisposition. Specifically, environments offering views (prospect) as well as a sense of enclosure (refuge) generate feelings of safety and pleasure. Compared with forest living, grasslands provided greater 'prospect' of seeing danger if it came as well as the opportunity for 'refuge' back in the forest, or amongst groups of trees separated by grassland. Very similar preferences have been reported in research from Europe, North America,

Japan and West and East Africa. Even people who have not been exposed to these landscapes show preferences for them over forest and desert scenes, suggesting the preference is a universal human instinct. Nevertheless, it is not as simple as the theory makes it sound. For example, safety may be less important than PRT suggests, since settings with good views (i.e. a high degree of prospect) and a low degree of refuge (tree cover) are preferred over settings with low prospect and high refuge. In addition, grasslands are not the only form preferred by humans, although features of prospect and refuge may make it easier to understand the landscape.

Preferences for natural settings seem to arise from two psychological motives, understanding and exploration. Understanding is about making sense of the visual scene, and needs the scene to have some structure that makes it legible and coherent, or easily interpreted, rather than formless. Exploration means that the visual scene contains additional information that can be discovered beyond the immediately visible. This is equivalent to extent in Attention Restoration Theory. It means an environment needs to have complexity and mystery, like a Japanese garden. Wilderness or wild settings are perceived negatively because they lack coherence and are difficult to understand, but they do offer greater opportunity for exploration. More managed rural settings are relatively easily understood but have less to explore. The visual configuration of grassland is openness, with small groupings of trees and an even ground surface. This configuration can be found in rural areas and on the edges of cities as well as in parks used for recreation. The features of grasslands represent moderate complexity and allow understanding and exploration.

Evolutionary theories, like PRT, suggest that the preference for grasslands subconsciously affects decisions people make about their surroundings, including preferences expressed in research studies. However, the theories cannot determine how people interact with their environment at any one time. For gardens and gardening, elements of evolutionary theories may play a small role. Obviously, open grassland is not the same as a home garden. However, on a domestic scale, garden designs often include different areas within a garden that allow for a feeling of enclosure as well as a sense of space. It could be that understanding and exploration are at least some part of motivations for gardening. After all, gardeners certainly talk about their gardens as places where there are always new things to see or to explore and say that gardening involves getting their garden to feel right, which may imply being able to understand it. They can create mystery by trying new things or changing the structure. Exploration and understanding also reinforce the potential for the garden as a place for recovery and reflection, or even flow, through fascination and extent, as well as being away and compatibility (see Chapter 3).

Last, the preferred park-like open grassland strongly resembles the physical form and aesthetic of 18th- and 19th-century landscaped gardens or parks, such as those created by landscape designers Capability Brown (1716–1783) and Humphry Repton (1752–1818). In these 'natural' settings, managed grassland areas are broken up by groups of trees, providing areas of shadow and shade. The aesthetic is also familiar from many landscape paintings of rural scenes showing clumps of trees with large leaf canopies, long views and low grasses and water. Smaller scale versions of these open grassy landscapes appear as public parks and gardens, and their essence is extracted in miniature for domestic gardens.

An alternative way to look at human–nature preferences is less to do with survival instinct and more to do with visual processing of the natural scene.

Fractals, perceptual fluency and affordance

Fractals

One way that visual perception offers a contribution to explaining landscape preferences is through considering *fractals*, specifically the fractal properties of outdoor scenes. Fractals are fragmented geometric shapes that can be split into parts, each of which is an exact replica of the whole, making multiple self-similar patterns. Fractals are common forms in nature, for example snowflakes, romanesco cauliflower or ferns. Fractal patterns are reproduced in architecture and can also be designed into environments and structures, for example in gothic cathedral architectures, or more recently Wolfgang Buttress' Hive sculpture (see Figure 4.1).[4] Experimental research has demonstrated that the most preferred outdoor scenes are scenes which do not produce self-similar patterns at either too high or too low a rate. This optimal fractal dimension turns out to coincide with grassland-like settings and, it is suggested, people's preference for them.[5] Fractals

Figure 4.1 An example of fractals in a structure: a section of 'Hive' by Wolfgang Buttress installed at Kew Gardens in 2016

have also been associated with restoration, because the repeated patterns make visual information more coherent and easier to process. This is known as perceptual fluency.

Perceptual fluency

Perceptual fluency[6] assumes that natural scenes are processed more fluently (easily) than urban or other types of settings because the visual system seems to be more tuned in to the organisation of visual information in natural scenes. This is possibly because they have fewer straight lines and sharp angles than constructed settings and are more coherent. In urban settings, the visual scene is less coherent, with variations of sizes, shapes, materials and so on. However, many suburban roads, avenues and crescents show how visual coherence can be designed into buildings and areas, contributing to perceptual fluency.[7] Easier processing makes lower demands on attention and so increases the possibility of renewing mental fatigue and restoration (see Chapter 3). The perceptual fluency account contributes to understanding how visual processing can determine landscape or natural preferences. Different garden styles may appear more visually fluent and thus encourage human engagement or restoration. Changes in garden style that favour more hard surfaces could reduce fluency and impact on perceived restorative quality.

Affordance

The concept of affordance[8] is that any environment is perceived as a set of object shapes and spatial relationships, which 'afford' possibilities for action. In a constructed world, handles are an affordance for opening doors or holding mugs. In the natural world, tree cover affords refuge. Action is dependent on the ability to make use of an affordance. Actions may initially be a reflex, like a baby's grasping reflex when presented with a finger, and an effective action then becomes a learned response. Affordances have to be learned in order to take the relevant social or cultural action to objects and places.

The idea of affordance emphasises the role of the environment in determining human actions, rather than the human survival instinct. For gardeners, objects and spatial relationships in their gardens may afford different actions for visitors or non-gardeners. Some gardeners may only rarely sit in their gardens, perhaps because for them gardens primarily afford physical action.

Rather than seeing human landscape preferences as instinctive, some researchers think that studies of preference may be tapping into a cultural bias. This cultural bias overlays any inbuilt preferences for grasslands. Equally, affiliation or fear responses to natural settings can be learned directly or from others and passed on through social contact. So, for example, parkland, or designed 'natural' landscape, has been incorporated in and around towns and cities over the past several hundred years and into the 21st century. This now-familiar landscape of parks and gardens is repeated in advertising images and visual media.[9]

Certainly, familiarity is a significant predictor of preference; the more familiar a physical setting, the more likely it is to be preferred. Similar preferences have been found for visual images of natural scenes in these commercial contexts as in research on ART,[10] reinforcing the cultural impact of our evolutionary past. Garden styles and preferences are culturally determined too, affected by history, social values and individual social status. So if gardening is working with nature, gardeners are trying not only to develop their own identities and personal preferences but also to manage the various social and cultural expectations of being a gardener in their own time.

Evolutionary and psychological approaches largely focus on the positive dimensions of the human–nature relationship to account for people's engagement with the natural world and their connectedness to nature. The positive aspects of the relationship are clearly highly motivating for gardeners. But, like any relationship, things may not always go so well. For people who are less interested in gardening, and who dislike or fear nature, the negative dimension of the relationship may loom large. The next section addresses the idea of collaboration with nature where nature takes an active role, and what happens if nature gets the upper hand.

WORKING WITH NATURE: 'IT'S GOT ITS OWN SORT OF PACE AND TIME WHICH IS VERY GROUNDING . . . YOU KNOW IT EXISTS AND YOU'VE GOT TO MANAGE IT'

Gardeners talk about working with nature and nature actively adding value to what they do. They get back twice or even ten times as much from their garden plot as they put in. The outcome of this reciprocal relationship with nature contributes to the person–place relationship, the sense of distinctiveness, self-worth and self-efficacy and of belonging, and contributes to identity as a gardener. Aspects of reciprocity, abundance, flowering and creativity are all the outcomes of an interaction between the individual's effort and nature's input. Gardeners can then show off the outcome of their creativity and effort as their plots transform across the seasons: as one plant or crop relinquishes the limelight, another one takes over.

The relationship clearly has two partners; they do not necessarily have the same goals at the same time. Things need be done in an ordered fashion in tune with nature; there is no sense in trying to beat nature, even if it can be frustrating on occasion: 'I think one of the most difficult things is not being able to hurry nature. I have been talking to the vine telling it to "hurry up"'.[11] Working in the garden or on the allotment means working with and attending to nature's time as well as managing time for the relationship. Time needs setting aside, and a balance has to be struck between how much time is needed and how much time can be given: 'It needs a lot more work than it gets from me'. Working with nature's time is particularly mentioned by allotment gardeners and suggests that successful plot-holding and productivity is a process of negotiating with nature through time. At some points, control is held by the individual and at others by nature. As presented by gardeners, the roles are as much emotional as practical.

Emotional aspects of the human–nature relationship in gardening are not only about personal identity, attachment to place or restoration and relaxation. The emotions are also about nature as enticing and fascinating; seeing seeds come up, though it's not a surprise, is still a thrill. Gardening provides feelings of giving life and a 'buzz', a relationship to be desired and sought out. Gardening also engages all the senses and is an embodied activity, reflected in the impassioned statements of how 'I am my garden':

> Something just happened, and that spring and summer I really enjoyed it and felt that I knew what I was doing and just felt an enormous empathy with the soil. I remember a really damascene moment of preparing the soil in March. I can remember the day vividly and I was just feeling the soil and feeling my hands going into it and just had this image of them as roots going on down and growing and just felt that was what I wanted.
>
> (Monty Don, garden writer and broadcaster, personal communication)

Monty Don's fabulous description of his transformative sense that he was (becoming) a gardener as he pushed his hands into the soil vividly expresses the physicality of what gardening – and the relationship with nature – can be. Being physically engrossed in the space, 'just you and your fork' listening to the birds, feeling the sun on one's back and 'pushing the spade in', all contribute to feelings of pleasure, enjoyment and peacefulness. This embodied experience of being outdoors gardening, doing something tangible, generates a sense of achievement, or self-efficacy, that expresses and reinforces their identity.

The actions and accompanying physical sensations involved in gardening provide access to embodied memories of past selves (see Chapter 2). One allotment holder, Tom, realised that when he was digging on his allotment he was making the same movements he had made as a 16-year-old shovelling coal into a furnace 50 years previously. To be suddenly aware of inhabiting his present and past selves at the same moment in his action can be a very powerful experience, especially in a banal task. As she has grown older, the writer Penelope Lively says that she particularly misses the physicality of what she calls 'intensive gardening' – digging, raking and hoeing. She describes herself at 80 as 'pottering and snipping' instead.[12]

Chapter 2 discusses how jobs in service of the garden are never ending. Any gardening manual or garden magazine demonstrates the range of actions that are needed to keep a garden in shape and that a garden might benefit from. An issue of *Gardeners' World* magazine (April 2017) lists how to grow tomatoes, organic pest control methods, pressure washers for paths and patios, and pruning for more flowers, as well as ways to improve the appearance of the garden by introducing dahlias or turning small spaces into a lush oasis. There is always something more to be done to meet their needs, improve their appearance or prevent them taking over.

In creating a garden, nature can definitely call the tune; the characteristics or voice of the plot and the plants have to be heard, and both plants and plot are active in determining how or whether the garden will work. The human gardener is not the only actor in the production of a garden. Even when starting from scratch, gardening is never simply a straightforward process of laying plans onto inert and docile landscape.[13] Nature will make itself felt.

> I spent ages digging out a fire pit and moving stone but then it rained so much that it flooded so I thought OK it wants to be a pond – I'll go with that.
>
> (Abz Love, 2016)[14]

The flood shifted the active role from the gardener to the elements in the garden and to nature. Gardening is not solely a process of domestication of nature through the practices of gardening. Actor Network Theory (ANT) gives the same status to all elements in the social situation, so plants, weather, nature, plans and gardeners would all be actors in the production of the garden. The theory is particularly concerned to put non-humans as actors or participants in the network.[15]

This position corresponds almost exactly to what gardeners describe as they work with nature and Abz Love's willingness to go along with the fire pit becoming a pond. Nature's intervention handed control to the pond as subject and object of action.

Plants too can be both the subject and object of action. For example, the ostensible purpose of trees is being attractive or green or colourful objects. They are actors, or subjects of action, because of their features, such as size, autumn colour or shape and because they also do other jobs, such as hiding the neighbour's shed or providing shade. As actors, plants actually 'draw the person down into their world and make for an understanding of their concerns and a commitment to their care',[16] a process which sounds like initiating flow. Sharing the roles makes the human–nature relationship a balancing act between two worlds, the human and the natural. The non-human actors in the garden change the human actors, generating an ongoing relationship, which is undoubtedly part of the attraction of gardening. It is reflected by gardeners' pleasure in anticipation of small changes; sometimes things happening in the garden or on the allotment are so exciting that gardeners can hardly wait for morning to see what has happened in their absence overnight.

Some of the caring aspect of gardening stems from the way that nature or objects (non-human objects) embody people, emotions and places: 'I don't know the names of all the plants but I know who or where they came from. That's what matters'. People frequently plant an identifiable living thing or install an object to commemorate a special event, person or pet. Gardens contain many plants or objects that remind gardeners of their travels or their other hobbies. It can be hard to leave these behind if they move, as Rosemary makes clear: 'I planted a shrub when each of my two children were born. When we moved, I wanted to dig them up and take them, but they were too big so I had to leave them and that was very hard'. Like the children, the shrubs had grown. Leaving the shrubs in the garden meant leaving the memories of being a parent and all that had gone on in that garden. Given that when people take over gardens they change things in order to create their own memories, Rosemary's gardening self could perhaps see a future where her children might cease to exist in the garden at all.

Humans and non-humans have a role to play in the garden to achieve a mutually beneficial outcome. Gooseberries or windchimes are tangible; memories are virtual or embodied. A successful relationship between gardener and garden clearly includes psychological support for human self-efficacy and identity. If the garden is given the time and space it needs, it will flourish too. When it is working well, the relationship relies on gardeners feeling able to maintain the challenges of working with nature's time, finding the time to complete the chores and to enjoy the production. If it becomes difficult to maintain their role in the partnership, identity could be affected.

Nature in control: 'Overwhelmed by my garden'

Gardening and being in touch with nature involves cultivation, taking care of the garden, nurturing living organisms and developing routines. The role of gardener relies on human persistence; managing the human–nature relationship is a continuous process of learning from success and from failure.

The view that 'gardens are cultural forms designed to shape and contain nature'[17] implies a biddable and potentially manageable form of nature. Unruly or undesirable elements such as poisonous plants and weeds and unwanted pests of all kinds can be excluded. But nature is powerful; it can be hard to contain and even harder to keep it in control. Gardening can sometimes feel like a Sisyphean task, or a serious long-term relationship, with a list of chores and a demanding partner. Much of the time spent outdoors gardening is in the constant management of nature, balancing the need to give it free rein to show off its talents, and to keep it under control, whether that requires starting from scratch, fencing the boundaries or laying traps for slugs and hanging birdfeeders. Managing nature is effectively a continuous tension between wanting to see songbirds in the garden and warning the pigeons off the strawberries. Gardeners who reported using more pesticides in their garden felt less in touch with nature, whereas gardeners who are interested in gardening for sustainability are likely to feel closer to nature and the environment through their actions. Perhaps the relationship with nature is conditional on the way that people interact with it, how they get the balance right for them.

The extent to which management is needed will depend on the type of garden or allotment, the gardener's favoured style or their gardening identity. Gardens are seen to be nature in a benign form; nature is not always benign or indeed bountiful. Gardeners are at the mercy of nature, and the concept of containment and human control is illusory. Doing domestic gardening at home or on the allotment, within the boundaries of suburbia, might not necessarily seem like keeping nature under control, but more like keeping irritants at bay. Nevertheless, the tasks vary depending on seasons, rainfall or other commitments. Going on holiday for a week in the growing season can mean bindweed has taken hold, and on return, the currant bushes and the leeks have to be freed if they are to thrive.

Even without extreme weather, nature in charge can be more threatening or unpleasant than the domestic gardening chores typically imply. Manicured or romantic ornamental and vegetable gardens can quickly go native and disappear under brambles and nettles. At times when other aspects of life have to take priority, and particularly as gardeners age, gardens become neglected. Chores such as weeding still need doing but become more difficult and can weigh heavy as a responsibility rather than part of a regular garden routine. Like Penelope Lively, older people may regret their lost capacity to do the physical work needed to care for their garden, to fulfil their part of the relationship, and this can impact on their sense of self-efficacy and their gardening identity.

The capacity of nature to engulf a garden can be alarming; getting it back into shape can be physically and emotionally challenging, sometimes actually stressful, making it difficult for a gardener to re-engage with their plot. It can be hard to achieve a sense of flow in untidy or dirty gardens; how much harder once a garden has become overwhelming. People need to be able to focus down, or be drawn down by the *fascination* inherent in natural settings and plants in order to become absorbed in the garden and achieve flow or *being away*. So for individual gardeners who do feel that nature is getting the upper hand, the opportunity for restorative potential may be reduced. In addition, in the life cycle of a garden, death and decay are more constant companions than the idea of the garden as an outdoor room of the family home might suggest. The connection between nature and decay or death as part of the human–nature relationship is less consciously acknowledged than the enjoyable and life-giving aspects of the relationship. However, if the relationship breaks down because the human partner is unable to play their part, nature as the dominant partner may cause people to feel depressed by their garden, rather than enthused. One of the reasons given by older people moving house into sheltered residential accommodation is that they no longer feel able to care for their gardens.

Nature can also be disgusting, scary and sometimes uncomfortable.[18] Having an innate predisposition to avoid some living things or places because they are dangerous is probably useful for survival. Certainly, nature or outdoors can be dangerous, dirty, home to bugs and to other sources of human disgust or fear, and people avoid it for those reasons. Walking in settings with high levels of refuge (enclosure), such as forests, is not as popular as walking in settings which have high prospect (views), such as countryside. Wilderness can be actively disliked and even inspire thoughts of death.[19] In fairy tales and in children's stories, scary things often happen in woods and forests, and parks, gardens and bushes can be perceived as frightening as well as exciting.[20] For people who are not enthused by nature, gardening is thus more likely to be seen as an unpleasant, uncomfortable sensory experience to be avoided.

There certainly are some unpleasant and dangerous elements of gardening, like dealing with wasps' nests and using power equipment, for instance. Mostly, the negative aspects of gardening are related to small scale activities and threats. Nevertheless, managing nature can have unfortunate consequences. Amongst the 27 million gardeners in the UK, there are about 87,000 injuries reported per year, due to care-lessness or accidents while gardening, most frequently falls (RoSPA figures, 2015). Men have more accidents than women, perhaps as a result of using dangerous garden tools and appliances to fulfil their responsibilities for specific jobs in the garden. Garden implements account for approximately 12,000 accidents per year, with lawnmowers and hedge trimmers, flowerpots and garden canes the main culprits. These are relatively small numbers, and deaths caused directly by gardening are very rare. The most recent death in the UK (2014) was due to contact with a poisonous plant. In countries with more poisonous species, fatalities are probably higher. Accidents are unlikely to discourage gardeners in the longer term because of the intrinsic reward of the gardening experience. However, the down-sides of the human–nature relationship mentioned by people less interested in gardening may deter them from starting at all.

In a market research survey of 1,000 people asking about their hobbies, the reasons for gardening were (predictably) relaxation, opportunities to be creative and contact with nature. There were more reasons given for not gardening. These included physical or practical aspects such as effort, time and hard work, the cost, lack of garden or not enough space to garden, children, which meant either that they had no time to dedicate to gardening, or that children took priority. Two other reasons given for not gardening were to do with nature: the weather, and its unpredictability, and being scared of bugs. Although most gardeners acknowledge the time and effort needed to do their garden, and they often complain about the weather, they are not put off by them. Nonetheless, talking to people who have given up gardening for long periods suggests that the time demands in particular can feel excessive, especially on an allotment: 'It felt like it had taken over my life'. Even where individuals felt strongly in touch with nature, the practicalities of keeping up the relationship became a vicious cycle. Because they were not spending enough time working on the plot, it became harder each time to make an impact. Making an active choice to hand over the allotment to someone else and stop gardening gave them freedom to enjoy nature in a different way, such as cycling, that was more compatible with their inclinations.

The human–nature relationship is only really a partnership to the extent that the elements can be shared by the actors in the garden and there is a match between the individual and the place. In Brisbane, Australia, residents who were more connected to nature gained greater benefits from being in their backyards (gardens) and interacted with the space more often and for longer periods, creating a virtuous circle of engagement with nature.[21] The jury is still out on whether being more connected to nature makes it more likely that someone will have contact with nature, or whether having contact with nature increases their feeling of connectedness.[22]

CONCLUDING REMARKS: WORKING WITH THE GARDEN

A predisposition for relationships with nature and preferences for open grassy landscapes may be innate and adaptive in survival terms. It is equally possible that survival is a result of a predisposition to avoid life threatening aspects of nature, such as scorpions or dense forest. Which of the predispositions is expressed in behaviour will depend on personal, social and cultural experience. Gardening, like any activity done in nature, could serve a fundamental biological need for connection with nature or it could be an expression of the connectedness to nature psychological trait. Whether it is fulfilling a biological or a psychological need, gardeners have a relationship with nature. The relationship allows both partners differing degrees of control in the production of the garden, reflecting elements of mastery, stewardship, participation and partnership. The physical, psychological and emotional work involved in the relationship is instrumental in developing and maintaining the gardening identity and attachment to place.

However, when nature takes over, gardens cease to offer compatibility and opportunities for fascination or extent, and identity may be threatened. The significance of maintaining their gardens for individual identity is echoed by what people say about being the gardener. If gardeners lose their sense of self-worth and distinctiveness, it impacts on their well-being, and they will need coping strategies to bolster self-esteem. In these situations, similar psychological benefits might be accessed by gardening in other ways. The value of gardening as a shared and therapeutic activity for health and well-being is the subject of the next chapter.

5

'IT KEEPS ME SANE'
Gardening as therapy

Paraphrasing Voltaire, take care of the garden and the garden will take care of you – and gardeners certainly say that gardening has been their salvation at times, keeping them sane. Personal accounts emphasise that at times of significant stress, such as problems at work or illness, gardening provides a means of coping: 'My husband was ill . . . I was fine but I had to come here, I had to come here [the allotment], this is where I was me'. In a study of gardeners with and without cancer, everyone (regardless of their health status) found that gardening provided an outlet for fear and worry about health. People described planting new shrubs and changing their garden in some way in response to receiving bad news about their own or their loved one's health. As they did so, the 'strenuous and creative work provided an outlet for fear, anger and frustration'.[1]

The health-giving properties of gardens and gardening have long been recognised. Previous chapters point to individual psychological development through gardening and the value of gardens and nearby nature as places for restoration and relaxation. A recent report[2] reviewing the evidence recommends gardening should be incorporated into policy by the National Health Service and Public Health England, and that local authorities and other providers should plan to make more land available for community and private gardens.

Gardening therapies have a long lineage, not least in the treatment of the insane at the early progressive Victorian private or county asylums in the UK, such as The Retreat at York, The Lawn in Lincoln or Mapperley Hospital in Nottingham. Walking in the grounds and gardens for women, and active gardening and agriculture or horticulture for men, was considered to be an important part of the therapy provided. The practice stemmed from a belief that outdoor exercise and gainful work was good for health generally and that it gave inmates a purpose and kept them occupied.

This chapter examines evidence for the value of gardening for gardeners and then considers the impact of therapeutic gardening programmes with individuals and groups. The chapter also considers the potential for nature's benefits beyond nearby nature in the garden, for example whether activity done outdoors has a similar or better effect on health and well-being than activity done elsewhere, and if so why.

IS GARDENING GOOD FOR YOU?

Gardeners report high levels of satisfaction with life, good physical activity levels and good psychological and physical health. These positive benefits have contributed to making gardening a means of improving other people's health and well-being. However, it could be that people who garden for themselves start out more positive, healthier and better able to manage their stress levels. Additionally, people who have access to private or shared gardens might be wealthier, older or better educated than people who do not (see Chapter 1). So to discover whether the benefits can be attributed to gardening, research needs to allow for these possible differences, or to compare gardeners with people who do not garden.

Comparing allotment gardeners and non-gardeners

A comparison of Dutch allotment gardeners and their home neighbours without an allotment showed that the allotment holders of all ages were more physically active than their neighbours.[3] The two groups were compared on levels of stress, life satisfaction, loneliness and contacts with friends. In terms of income, education, gender and stressful life events in the past year, there was no difference between younger people with and without an allotment garden. Older allotment holders only differed inasmuch as they were healthier and more satisfied with life compared with their non-gardening neighbours. Allotment gardening is therefore associated with a healthier lifestyle and greater physical activity, particularly benefitting older people. Nevertheless, it is possible that only people already most actively engaged in their allotments took part, or that younger people may seek more or less active forms of stress-relieving behaviours than gardening.

In a UK study comparing allotment holders and non-gardeners, gardeners' self-esteem and mood improved between the start and end of a session on their allotment, and scores for anxiety and depression went down (though no one was clinically anxious or depressed to start with).[4] How long they had owned the plot, how long they spent there or the amount of gardening done in the past week were not reasons for the positive effect. On average, the non-gardeners weighed more than the gardeners, and gardeners had higher self-esteem, higher energy and lower depression and fatigue than non-gardeners. Comparison of Japanese allotment holders and non-gardeners showed that the gardeners had better physical and mental health.[5] They also ate more vegetables, but drank more alcohol, than the non-gardeners. There were no differences between them on weight and height, or on nature-relatedness scores. On average, the gardeners went to their allotments about ten times per month, spending at least an hour there each time. Even if they went only once a week for a short time, the health outcomes were the same. Both these studies demonstrate that even a single, short allotment session can be beneficial for existing allotment holders and support the notion of gardening as an intervention.

People in the Japanese study said that the main reason for going to their allotment was for a mental break. Reasons for the positive effect of gardening sessions could be the chance to switch off in contact with nature, or aspects of being away, fascination and compatibility or the opportunity to achieve flow or mindfulness (see Chapter 3). Allotment holders enjoy being outdoors having contact with nature and the sense of achievement from taking home and eating the vegetables they have just harvested. They look to their garden as an opportunity for restoration and stress relief as well as social interaction, and being active is important. The opportunity for older people to increase their levels of sociability is mentioned in several allotment gardening projects. The reported benefits refer to the social and psychological dimensions of place attachment and Identity Process Theory (see Chapter 2); in particular the sense of achievement boosts self-efficacy, and working on their own allotment gives individual distinctiveness.[6]

So for gardeners, it appears that gardening may be a more effective way to relieve stress than other kinds of activity. This was actually tested in a study of gardeners on their allotments to see whether light gardening or reading magazines was most effective at recovery from stress following a demanding computer task. The magazines were screened for any nature content, and light gardening meant pruning plants and bushes, weeding, and sowing and planting on their own allotment. Stress was measured by cortisol levels (a stress-related hormone), which went down for everyone from the end of the stressful task to the end of the reading or gardening activity. It went down most in the group who gardened. The reading group's mood went down after their reading task, whereas the gardening group reported an uplift in mood after their gardening activity, emphasising the benefit of engaging in a gardening session. However, preventing some of the gardeners from gardening while they were on their allotment probably contributed to the lowered mood in the reading group, even though their stress did go down.[7]

For older community-dwelling adults able to make active choices about their leisure time, gardening may be one of several hobbies. Looking at motivations for leisure and for participation in a gardening scheme in a group of older people, the most important motivators were fitness, creativity and intellectual growth. Friendship, social esteem and need for calm or to relieve stress were not strong motivators.[8] Of course, for people who are taking part in leisure activities, lower motivation for stress relief may mean they are already less stressed. Socio-emotional Selectivity Theory[9] proposes that as people age, or as the future becomes more scarce (e.g. through illness), they are more likely to devote their time to activities and relationships that promote positive feelings. They are more likely to see the good in things, for example to pick out the positive aspects of an image rather than negative ones, and for people who are able to pursue activities they enjoy, other stressful aspects of their lives recede, resulting in lower perceived stress.

So gardening is good for healthy people who already garden. The question is whether the effect is as positive for non-gardeners or unhealthy people. The next section looks at some examples from the substantial number of therapeutic gardening programmes, (re-)introducing people to gardening, specifically related to mental health and well-being. It briefly reviews the evidence for the positive impact of

Figure 5.1 The allotment site in the June sunshine

gardening on the health and psychological well-being of individuals and groups.

GARDENING AS THERAPY

The aim of therapeutic gardening depends on whether programmes are designed for health, meaning mostly physical health, or for therapy. Horticultural therapy is a form of occupational therapy. Activities of gardening including planting, sowing seeds, raking and sweeping up leaves are directed towards achieving some particular clinical goal, such as improving mobility. Therapeutic horticulture, more often called social and therapeutic horticulture, is concerned with more generalised improvement in individual well-being, through the same types of gardening activities. People can take a more or less active role in activities, or have a passive role, such as sitting and looking at the garden, for example. Therapeutic intervention programmes have similarities with community gardening projects, the main differences being that key members of a community instigate those schemes, and that their projects are intended to be inclusive of everyone in a specific community location, rather than driven by a defined psychological or physical need (see also Chapter 6).

Social and therapeutic horticulture has been offered to people with a range of disadvantages or disabilities. The range includes those with mental health problems, dementia, learning disabilities, physical ill-health or disabilities, and marginalised groups such as young offenders, refugees, asylum seekers and victims of torture. Unlike domestic gardening, therapeutic gardening usually takes place in a shared space, such as an allotment. The purpose of therapeutic projects is to support people, and their effectiveness is based on the outcomes reported by them, rather than formal measurements of behaviour or mood. Individuals who feel better as a result of gardening might need less medication; they have somewhere to go every day, where they have people to talk to. Thus, the project has had a significant impact on their experience. For the person, experience at a garden project can increase their sense of self-worth (self-esteem) and offer psychological benefits for their individual identities and their sense of belonging.

The benefits of gardening-based programmes for improving mental health are consistently supported by evidence. The programmes can be farm-based, allotment-based projects, emphasise skills training and development or be created for particular groups or circumstances. Gardening-based therapies and horticultural therapy have benefits for people experiencing a range of chronic mental health issues, including depression and psychosis.[10] The positive outcomes for the individuals who take part in these interventions are that they are treated as and see themselves as individuals, rather than as patients or clients; they are supported by the presence of other people; and having work to do with a purpose, which involves tending and cultivating plants, helps them to develop self-efficacy and self-esteem.

Therapeutic gardening projects are not only about mental health. For fathers taking part in an allotment group, the opportunity it gave for shared occupation was important and offered them a way to share masculine parenting activity. It also allowed them to form stronger relationships with their young children.[11] For refugees and for other marginalised groups, gardening can be linked to identity processes, particularly self-efficacy and self-esteem, and providing opportunities for personal continuity. It also links to the dimensions of occupation of 'being a gardener' (see Chapter 2). As well as gardening, support can include opportunities to take part in other therapies offered at the garden site, such as art therapy and relaxation, or practical sessions to help improve coping strategies and the chances of future employment for example. People become attached to the gardens during the therapy process, and the emotional bonds formed with the place are constructive in helping clients resolve personal issues. The concept of a caring environment that offers opportunities to gain support from others in the same place, and to provide caring for plants and other humans, reinforces the value of nature as a co-therapist in resolving personal issues.

Activity on a small scale is effective too. An experimental programme of 12 classes on growing and tending provided for a group of older adults led to a significant improvement in well-being after the programme. Making gardens available and supported gardening in care settings benefit the physical and mental well-being of people with dementia and terminal illnesses. Being able to see the garden and being active in it can reduce agitation, and the sensory experience of being in the garden can increase relaxation. One of the ways that it seems to work, according to carers,[12] is through remembrance of past selves and competence as a gardener while having contact with plants, as well as the restorative value of being away, or having a change of scene. The garden environment is mentally undemanding, as Attention Restoration Theory suggests, it is visually coherent, and it can provide information about place and purpose.

It is hard to establish which elements of the many programmes are of most value in predicting good outcomes for individuals. Attention Restoration Theory proposes that the natural world is restorative, that nature has the potential for restoration from directed attention fatigue and from other demands, allowing reflection and recovery. Comments from members of therapeutic gardening programmes certainly refer to experiences like being away, fascination and compatibility. Other benefits of therapeutic gardening experiences that have been identified include the sense of freedom and space associated with being outside in nature; the social engagement with others; issues relating to work and employment; physical activity, health and well-being; and the development of self confidence and self-esteem.[13] As the previous chapters have shown, these features are not limited to therapeutic projects; they represent what gardeners say about their experience and why gardening appeals to them. The features indicate how gardening is a key means of achieving distinctiveness and feelings of doing something meaningful, known as authenticity, and discussed as part of identity development. Therapeutic projects suggest that people who have not gardened before become engaged with it through the projects because at least one of the elements fulfils a psychological need, drawing out part of themselves they had not previously been aware of or able to express. It remains to be seen whether gardening suits everyone.

At least some of the pleasure of gardening is being in contact with nature, the visual aesthetic and relaxation, which are also present in public gardens and parks. Does visiting gardens have the same effect as gardening?

Garden visiting: 'I love going and looking round gardens as well'

Garden visiting is very popular. Motivations for visiting historic and special interest gardens across the UK include having a nice day out and enjoying a garden. It also provides a source of ideas for people's own gardens. Other reasons for visiting are social or garden-specific, such as particular planting or settings and being with people who share their interests. The responses to visitor surveys identify that there is some overlap between gardening and garden visiting in terms of benefits. There has been some research looking at this. In the US, 300 visitors (almost all of them were gardeners) to three botanic gardens in Florida were assessed for mood (depression), stressful life events and how stressed they felt at the start and end of their visit. The results showed that the visitors felt less stressed at the end of the visit than at the start. Although no one was actually suffering from depression at the time, the visit was most effective for people who scored higher on the depression scale (meaning that their mood was lower at the time). This was a short-term improvement based on one visit, but it endorses the potential for stress reduction in a garden setting for gardeners at least.[14] It does not confirm whether the same effects would be found for non-gardeners. The evidence from gardening therapy programmes suggests that it probably would.

Looking at what people do or feel while they are on their visits provides some insights into why visits may be beneficial. In interviews with self-confessed keen gardeners (ages 60–81 years) while they walked through parks and public gardens on a visit, they too made links between their own gardens and where they were visiting. The gardeners referred to being present in the moment and being able to de-stress by watching what was happening in the garden. The possibilities for getting ideas, learning about new or different plants and being part of a gardening community were also valued. For gardeners, the benefits of their own garden are mirrored in visiting other gardens, as Attention Restoration Theory would predict for gardeners and non-gardeners alike. It is further evidence, if it were needed, for the value of gardens as a therapeutic environment.

Community gardening projects

The UK City Farms and Community Gardens Federation includes as community gardens 'tiny wildlife gardens to fruit and vegetable plots on housing estates or large community polytunnels'. Community gardens can be located in specific settings such as hospitals or schools and might host therapeutic programmes and support other local groups through outreach work or educational programmes on-site. Community gardening projects are distinct from allotment gardening in the UK, and from private gardening, by being collective and open to the public in their local area. In the US and Canada (and elsewhere), community gardens are similar to allotments. They have a broad remit: enabling groups to grow produce to sell or members of the community to grow vegetables for personal use. They can provide local residents with opportunities to improve the local environment, and in some cases, directly address social problems such as anti-social behaviour. For example, in one city, a community-based grassroots initiative was developed to transform an area of fly-tipping, and a community garden was set up by the council and a health agency to promote the health and environmental benefits of gardening.[15]

Community gardens projects very often developed as a catalyst to address social problems or neighbourhood issues. Having seen that unused space could be used as a garden, residents (alone or in conjunction with other agencies) start to colonise it, talk to other people about it and transform it from wasteland to productive plots. The outcome of the collective action extends beyond the garden project itself, to increased civic engagement, because individuals have to become involved with planning and legal authorities over issues of ownership and management (see Chapter 6). In addition, the activities can increase personal access to social capital through the use of social networks and access to new skills or education and change individuals' sense of identity. Volunteering in the garden may lead to employment opportunities elsewhere. Thus, the remit of community gardening is different to therapeutic gardening, but can deliver similar outcomes for individuals. Very similar benefits have been highlighted from community gardening projects in the US, that is, social capital, positive health outcomes and personal motivations such as time to enjoy nature and opportunities to socialise as well as dietary change and food production.[16] These outcomes are comparable with the findings of other gardening projects and schemes.

Having examined the evidence for the benefits of gardening, for existing gardeners or for people who have previously not gardened, the conclusion has to be that gardening, and contact with nature in the garden, has positive impacts for individual mental health and well-being. But the key question remains whether it is specific to gardening. That is, due to the activity of gardening, or whether it is contact with nature in the garden that is having the effect, or indeed both. There is also a question of whether the contact with nature or the social dimension of the projects drives the benefits, particularly in rural community projects where nature is already a given.

Elements identified as resulting from therapeutic gardening can be gained from other activities in nature, and it is not only home gardens and allotment gardens or garden projects that afford the factors of being away, extent, and (soft) fascination and compatibility or the opportunities for flow. At least part of the explanation for the positive effect of gardening is the evidence for the value of nearby nature and exposure to outdoor natural settings. The next section reviews findings that show similar psychological benefits from other activities undertaken in nature or natural settings, including having natural views from windows or images of natural settings.

NATURE, THE ENVIRONMENT AND HEALTH

Founding evidence for the potential of nature to impact physical health in a valuable and cost-effective way came in the form of a natural experiment.[17] Using hospital data on recovery outcomes for patients who had been in wards with a view of greenery from their window (natural view) or of a wall (urban view), it was demonstrated that patients with the natural view needed less pain relief following surgery and recovered in less time compared with those with the view of a brick wall. The benefits of greenery or green views for recovery was also shown in a Korean study[18] in a hospital where patients were randomly assigned to either a room with plants or without them. The patients in the room with potted plants had shorter stays in hospital and needed less pain relief medication than those without plants. In both cases, because the patients were randomly assigned and because the analysis was of data routinely collected by the hospital, the improved recovery rates can be directly attributed to the rooms with green views or potted plants.

Research into the human benefits of nature done over the past 50 years confirms that different types of contact with nature and outdoor natural environments promote health and well-being. The evidence supports physiological benefits from interaction with nature (such as lower blood pressure), restoration and recovery of directed attention fatigue and from stress, nature-based therapeutic interventions, favourite places as restorative and higher satisfaction with life associated with being close to nature. Contact with nature can improve psychological well-being specifically, by increasing positive mood, reducing depression and improving cognitive functioning,[19] and connectedness to nature is associated with greater interest in the outdoors. It becomes increasingly obvious why policy makers are urged to make more green spaces available and why doctors are prescribing nature-based activity to improve physical activity and psychological well-being.

Exercise

Research comparing outdoor and indoor exercise shows that directly after the session, exercising outdoors was associated with greater feelings of positive engagement, greater energy and lowered levels of tension, anger and depression.[20] Experimental investigations demonstrate that exercise done on a treadmill indoors while able to see images of pleasant scenes improved self-esteem more than exercise without them. Unpleasant scenes actually had a negative effect on self-esteem, and unpleasant rural scenes had the greatest negative impact on mood. Unpleasant rural scenes are apparently more disturbing than urban ones, perhaps because of differing expectations of the two environments. The study concluded that 'green exercise' had implications for public health, and further studies demonstrated that, like allotment sessions, the best 'dose' of green exercise for mental health is short engagements, and that the presence of water increases the effect. Most encouragingly, these studies show greater effects on self-esteem for younger participants and greatest effects for those with poorer mental health.

Data collected for a Scottish health survey[21] showed that regular use of natural settings for physical activity, such as woodlands, parks and beaches, was better for mental health. Regular use of sports pitches or gyms and even using outdoor settings less than once a week were all positively associated with well-being scores, compared with not using these environments. Although causal links are not clear – those with better mental health may be more willing or able to do exercise outside – data from a general population and an everyday setting provides valuable evidence of the potential of natural settings for physical activity, and for improving health and well-being.

Walking

Walking in green (rural) and blue (coastal) natural environments can improve mood and stress levels. Walking as part of the daily commute to work can be a positive way to improve physical fitness and bring people into contact with nearby nature for instorative experiences. However, walking through green spaces on its own, while good for physical health, is not automatically restorative; people need to actively engage with the natural environment by noticing what they are passing or hearing.[22] As well as allowing 'being away' (see Chapter 3), the aerobic activity of walking increases blood flow, including to the brain, which may help walkers to focus on problems.

Nearby nature and health

Nearby nature (street trees, public gardens and parks) has a positive effect on attention restoration, so greening the urban and suburban environment is healthier for everyone as well as making it more appealing to residents, walkers, runners and commuters. The higher the density of trees in an urban environment, the better the health of residents. Having only 11 more trees in a city block can have a health impact equivalent to an increase in personal income of $20,000 and the commensurate reduction in cardiovascular risk.[23] Nearby nature helps to deliver this health impact, offering walkers and others the opportunity for positive psychological benefits of lowered cortisol levels and improved physical fitness.[24]

Nature and health: how does it work?

Several mechanisms are proposed for the link between nature and health,[25] of which stress reduction is the most obvious and the most strongly evidenced. Psychological (mood, restoration) and physiological (cortisol or blood pressure) measures assessed in or following exposure to natural settings show a reduction in stress levels and an increase in positive mood. Other obvious mechanisms are via physical activity and improved air quality. Exercise is good for health wherever it is done, but the willingness to undertake exercise is largely intrinsically motivated, people want to exercise for its own sake. The evidence from short sessions of exercise clearly shows that natural settings boost the effects of exercise in the short term and should have the same effect each time. Moreover, natural settings or green spaces are not always about active leisure, they may afford passive activity like sitting and enjoying the view, which is relaxing and enjoyable in itself. Furthermore, evidence for the benefits of green space in run-down areas of large cities and in more affluent areas includes positive effects for improved community cohesion (see also Chapter 6). Whether or how this affects health is less clear.

Time spent in contact with nature can have physiological effects by lowering arousal (e.g. reducing blood pressure), which is good for health. Time spent in nature is also associated with a greater sense of well-being, arising from taking pleasure in things which are aligned with personal values and which make people feel intensely alive and authentic (known as eudaimonic well-being).[26] This particular sense of well-being is attuned to the idea of identity or compatibility (see Chapters 2 and 3) and relates to both gardening and other forms of activity in nature, such as exercise. In addition, increased connectedness to nature makes people subjectively happier (known as hedonic well-being).[27] It would appear therefore that despite some of the downsides of gardening discussed in Chapter 4, gardening is good for us, including for our health. The question of whether nature or gardening is most beneficial for those who already feel closer to nature remains a thorny one.

CONCLUDING REMARKS: GARDENING IS GOOD FOR YOU!

The material reviewed in this chapter leaves no doubt that gardens, gardening and having contact with nature can, as gardeners say, keep people sane. There is sufficient evidence for the positive impact of exposure to nature, gardening projects, and horticultural therapies on individual and community mental health. The evidence that gardening is good for gardeners is unassailable. Gardening gets people outdoors, it involves physical exercise and can lead to increased fruit and vegetable consumption. Together with the evidence for opportunities to raise activity levels, improve awareness of the environment and the possibilities for social benefit by doing activities in nature, social prescribing of gardening is now strongly recommended. Perhaps then, gardening will save lives.

Because many activities are either always done outdoors in nature, or can be done in nature, gardening is not the only way to keep sane; walking, running and cycling as well as camping, sailing or climbing can all put people in touch with the natural world, where they can harvest the measurable benefits and achieve flow. The best results are for people who already garden or who are more connected to nature, and this suggests that being connected to nature is a necessary condition for engaging with activities in natural settings.

Gardening is all about being engaged directly in the nature at hand, and this distinguishes gardening from other activities in nature. However, it is not a one-way process. Having contact with nature may increase people's interest in it and thus raise people's feeling of connectedness, as the therapeutic horticulture programmes suggest. If people do not have access to nature, how can they benefit? Using images and simulations has already shown some impact for frail, elderly people in care homes, and passive activity such as being able to see and enjoy green views or nearby nature from the window is still restorative; sitting in a pop-up park below the office is even better.

So far, exploring the attention-holding power of the garden, and the gardening experience, has largely focused on the individual gardener, their identity and attachment to place. The final chapter reflects on what has emerged in this exploration of the gardening experience and then addresses some of the themes that have sprung up along the way. These include age and gender, and gardening career and expertise, together with gardening as opportunity for resistance. In conclusion, I reflect on gardening as a form of occupation.

6

TAKING UP OR TAKING OVER?
Reflections on gardening as an occupation

The garden is a focus for psychological processes relating to person and place. To examine the psychology of gardening, each chapter has focused on one of the consistent and interlinked themes that have emerged from research about gardeners and gardening. The themes represent gardeners' own words about the enchanting, absorbing and physical experience of being in and doing the garden. In addressing the themes, a number of mostly psychological theories and concepts have been described that illustrate the complexity of gardening as an everyday leisure activity. Personal practices in gardens and gardening draw on prevailing concepts of nature, ageing and gender, for example that society needs to find ways to sustain the natural environment or that older people should remain active. These views in turn inform what gardeners say and what researchers say about it.

This final chapter begins by reflecting on psychology and gardening, and the subsequent section examines the relevance of gender, age and the gardening career. Discussion of gardens as sites of resistance, and guerrilla gardening, is followed by an exploration of being a gardener in the 21st century. This includes an observation on expertise and the role of the media as well as raising issues that affect gardening in a changing society. The chapter concludes by exploring the notion of gardening as occupation.

PSYCHOLOGY AND GARDENING

The issues addressed in this book are inevitably a partial picture of the psychology of gardening. There are many other aspects of gardening and of psychology that have not been included, for example the power of individual plants to affect mood or behaviour. In seeking evidence of psychology for gardening, I might have expected to uncover research into why people choose certain types of garden or have particular plant preferences. Aside from the manicured/romantic distinction (Chapter 2) and environmental identity and gardening practices, there is limited detailed psychological evidence on these areas of individual or cultural differences in gardening, despite my lucky break in that Sunday newspaper experiment. There is a degree of distinction between a psychology of gardening and a psychology of gardens. The focus here has been on psychological processes that might explain why *gardening* is so motivating.

Psychological explanations for human functioning tend to work on the basis that behaviour is the result of an interaction between what is innate or biologically determined and what is learned from the past and current environment, which is a product of human cultural endeavour. So although there may be a possible human predisposition to approach or avoid nature, as biophilia/biophobia suggests, gardeners are part of a community that attributes value to gardens and gardening. This social value is transmitted via shared activities, doing chores on your grandparents' allotment for example. These practices then influence whether someone is more or less connected to nature, rather than it being solely an innate disposition.

People identify strongly with their gardens and appreciate them as spaces for freedom of expression. Aspects of self-identity can be made visible through gardening and the creation of place. Gardening fulfils human psychological needs, which determine how the garden looks or what the gardener does to express a need for structure, or their environmental identity. In doing so, they form attachments to the garden as a place. Opportunities for creativity and for self-efficacy through gardening give people a sense of purpose and achievement, of authenticity in their identity as a gardener. Gardening schemes can build social networks, extend opportunities for work and improve individuals' physical and mental health. The positive impact of gardening is due to the restorativeness of the environment and being in touch with nature as well as the chance to achieve flow in the garden. Opportunities to be mindful in the garden can also reduce stress. Theories underpinning the benefits relate to the interaction between person, psychological processes and place. The human–nature relationship played out in the garden contrasts the idea of nature as in need of human management and control, with the idea of reciprocity, which gives an active role to nature as a gardener. Who has the leading role may depend on psychological need or gardening style.

Working in the soil, sowing and planting, and other actions by the gardener, change nature. The effect on nature is visible in the appearance of flowers or vegetables that were not present in the garden before the gardener was there. Equally, the gardener removes parts of nature, to make space for new versions of it. This is not the same as running or climbing. The same embodied sensations of being outdoors in nature, the restorative aspects of soft fascination and pleasure of achieving flow are present in those activities, but their primary purpose is not to deliberately intervene in the environment. The processes related to place are therefore different, and so a person's relationship with their garden as a place will be different from attachments to other natural settings or nearby nature.

Gardening is a testament to human agency. Gardens are also sites of cultural consumption and class. So, as well as identity, aspects of gender, age, income and work status are all relevant. The following section discusses three dimensions of gardening that have emerged in several of the chapters, gender, age and the notion of a gardening career, and then reflects on the notion of gardens as sites of empowerment and resistance.

GENDER, AGE AND THE GARDENING CAREER

The predominance of women in gardening research reflects the demography of gardening in the UK, which shows that more than half of people identifying as doing gardening are women (57% in the UK). Why is this? Women and men have similar motives for wanting to garden and rate being creative as a key reason. Women tend to value aspects such as respecting themselves, developing skills and being alone with their thoughts more highly and see these as more satisfying aspects of gardening than men do. Men, on the other hand, prize peace of mind, enjoying nature and independence and self-reliance more highly, but these are small differences. However, only women considered feelings of mastery as a satisfying aspect of gardening.

One explanation for more women doing gardening is that it offers them a means of empowerment.[1] The garden provides a room of their own, a space to take control and express themselves, within a domestic setting outside the house and removed from the duties that belong there. The space still involves a form of caring work, but it is under their own control, or at least they get to negotiate with nature on their own terms. Gardening is still gendered to an extent; women gardeners talk about sharing out the tasks, with men called upon for heavier physical work, wielding machinery and mowing lawns: 'It's more my thing, although he does the real heavy digging stuff and I just do the nice things'.

Even if help is enlisted, women will take overall responsibility for decisions about the garden (especially allotments), expressed repeatedly in statements that they are 'the gardener', implying that the other tasks are not really gardening. In taking over the garden, and doing everything, women are challenging not only their partners (or families) for space and time, but also supposedly outdated ideas of outside as a masculine domain, and inside as the natural feminine domain of care, in the service of family or others.[2] By prioritising outdoor garden and allotment caring and creativity over inside duties, therefore, gardens are sites of resistance and an opportunity to demonstrate women's empowerment. As more young people take up gardening, it remains to be seen how 21st-century attitudes affect their experience.

Gardens as places of resistance and empowerment can also be seen in community gardening projects. Roles and responsibilities allocated and offered to community members often prompt gendered assumptions that men should help with the heavy jobs and lifting. But women quickly made clear that they can do and enjoy these tasks. Skills, knowledge and expertise also determined who does what in the garden, and women who acted to initiate a garden project often became leaders or co-leaders of the collective gardening team. Taking on a shared leadership role included being sensitive and flexible about other people's constraints, whereas male leadership was seen as being more directive.[3] Women particularly valued the socialising opportunities of community gardening, as a mix of work and leisure, and giving access to other contacts in neighbourhoods for example. The garden allowed women to exercise their own power and the freedom to develop their identities, outside the automatic division of labour by gender. In doing so, they could take pride and pleasure in the often-demanding work involved, and were able to make use of and to resist gender stereotyping, by being more socially and person-oriented in leadership style but also doing the heavy lifting.

Gardeners work 'at' as well as 'on' their gardens. Gardening is work, whether in the community, on the allotment or at home. It's an occupation. It carries a range of responsibilities and routines: 'You've got to remember that you're not just there looking at flowers . . . you're out there for one purpose . . . it's always work orientated' and requires orchestration of the different roles for humans and for nature and inanimate objects like garden ornaments. Gardening is time consuming as well as time shifting, to be juggled with other responsibilities, including families. Vegetable gardening creates more work of cleaning, preparing, cooking and storage. People take up gardening for interest, for pleasure or to fulfil a need and then they are 'hooked'. They can start small and need little more than willingness to try; special skills or greenfingers are not necessary. Gardening is a 'job for life', with no natural end point or retirement age; once you have started, you can just carry on. The garden carries on regardless.

Gardening projects for children in schools and in the community instil an interest in growing things and are effective in improving diet and environmental awareness, especially for young people who do not have gardens at home. Exposure to nature in childhood makes it more likely that adults will participate in nature-based activities.[4] So early exposure to gardening can spark an interest, which can be revived if the inclination or opportunity arises. Gardeners report that they really only got hooked on gardening when they had a place of their own to garden, so having a plot, or pots, is essential. But they had probably gardened in some form before then or done other things which took them into contact with nature (Chapter 2). Spending on gardens by 20–34-year-olds doubled between 2010 and 2014, so the UK at least might continue to be a 'nation of gardeners'. Almost half of all garden purchases are made through supermarkets. Picking up plants, bulbs and seeds in supermarkets may be a good way for people to try out gardening since it reduces the perceived pressure to demonstrate expertise, for example in garden centres.

Being greenfingered (or green thumbed) implies that only some people would be good gardeners, but there is little evidence that this is so. People who are more connected to nature might be more interested in gardening; that does not mean they are better at it, only that they are more willing to persist. Indeed, starting to garden could lead to feeling more connected to nature. The visitor to other people's gardens tends to see the successes, the evidence for greenfingers, whereas gardeners remember the trials and the failures; paradoxically, gardeners are unlikely to describe themselves as greenfingered.

Many currently older gardeners might have been gardening for years. Whether they have or not, whenever they are gardening they bring their younger selves with them, together with any experiences of being in the garden (see Chapter 4). As people age, opportunities to garden and the sense of contentment and creativity gained from it may increase. Gardening can provide a way of resisting the notion that ageing is a process of declining capacities. People can actively choose to continue their hobby or to take it up for the first time, supporting valued aspects of their identity and sense of self-worth, and keeping physically fitter[5]. Older gardeners typically have experience and knowledge they can share, so they can be a resource for younger or novice gardeners on the allotment or in the family, or working in neighbourhood garden schemes. Being able to support others is another way to express their gardening identity and self-esteem as well as a chance to create connections to future generations. Keeping up the garden, or helping others to do so, can demonstrate how they are keeping occupied, taking responsibility for themselves and their environment.

While they can still garden, older gardeners are happier and healthier than people who don't garden, though they may regret their inability to fully engage in some physical tasks, moving from digging to snipping: 'I'll try and carry on as long as I can, I do have the manual help now with the boys'. However, leaving a garden behind or becoming unable to garden can be an emotional experience. Being unable to fulfil the gardening role because of illness, for example, can lead to feeling restricted by the garden together with a sense of bereavement at the loss of purpose or occupation, of place and of identity.[6] For people who move house or actively decide to stop gardening, no longer having to meet expectations of keeping up the garden can be a relief, and the sense of restriction can be lifted. If they can retain some aspects of having a garden, such as access to an outside space, some pots or a shared garden space that can provide hands-on contact with nature and the sense of freedom that they enjoy, older people can still resist the notion of decline. Looking out at a view over a garden and engaging with the sights and sounds of nearby green space can still be restorative and energising (instorative).

GARDENING AS RESISTANCE – TRANSCENDING BOUNDARIES

So gardens can be empowering, and they can be places of resistance for women, older people and communities. Community projects are driven by the needs of a neighbourhood as a collective entity, taking direct action in order to address local issues of alienation. Community gardens typically occupy spaces that would not otherwise be gardens. They are achieved through grassroots action, by taking over and reclaiming abandoned public or derelict private land. The aim of the garden is empowerment of communities and inclusivity, achieved by transforming the space into somewhere communities want to engage with, to grow plants and produce, to beautify city spaces.

In Liverpool, the remaining residents of a run-down, dilapidated area of the city (Granby) began to resist the decay by reclaiming the outside spaces as a community garden. They started cleaning up the streets, collected the rubbish and brought out potted plants from their houses, and put their garden furniture on to the street. They were undertaking acts of 'communing' by sharing their private domestic homes with the street and with others. The residents also painted empty buildings and encouraged plants to grow up their walls. The activity generated by the residents can be described as 'guerrilla gardening'.[7] There was a parallel adult education programme on ecology and gardening running in a vacant plot, but this organised activity did not lead to the community action. The activists themselves said that they were working in public space and not behind railings.

The definition of a garden is that it occupies an enclosed or boundaried space. This implies exclusion; some people are inside while others are kept out. So in resisting the privilege of enclosure, community gardens and guerrilla gardening are intended to be boundary-free and inclusive. Ironically, however, as the Granby Street activists pointed out, schemes that initially champion inclusivity and open access can become closed.[8] Often with the best intentions, such as security, restrictions are put in place. These can be physical enclosure by fencing and locked gates, which privilege access for some (with keys) and not others. Alternatively, restriction can be by people and by rules generated by the group that decides and polices who and what is allowed in the gardens. This may inadvertently favour values and practices that reflect existing inequalities and divisions between those who feel part of the community garden and those who do not. In these situations, it is likely that the benefits of gardening do not accrue to everyone. But there can be other ways to resist or to create garden spaces out of nothing.

Guerrilla gardening is like community gardening in that it involves cultivating someone else's land, but it is more surreptitious, planting or sprinkling seeds at night without permission from the landowner. This can be a radical act, filling in the margins, little spaces that exist everywhere and turning them into tiny oases, or using planting that is typically weeded out, like dandelions or chickweed. The great thing about guerrilla gardening is that anyone can do it; it is easy and it doesn't take long. Using seed bombs or grenades containing mixtures of seeds and growing medium and fertiliser, the planting can be delivered to its location targeted at different flowering points, to green up city areas.

The original London guerrilla gardener, Richard Reynolds, was described as an inspiration to a new generation of gardeners in a listing of most influential gardeners. This kind of activity makes gardening more obviously exciting, rather than relaxing, and could be influencing younger people to think about gardening. Another example of guerrilla gardening is The Pansy Project, a very specific form of horticultural resistance as an artistic project and personal campaign, which plants pansies at sites of homophobic abuse and attacks. In this project, the outcome is a gallery of images online that commemorate the abusive attacks.[9] The ability to share guerrilla garden sites, and to challenge abuse, through social media and the internet also extends the boundaries of gardens in the way intended by their creators.

By growing over the neighbours' fence or onto the street, gardens also resist their boundaries. Gardens do not have to be conventional or enclosed to provide psychological benefits, despite the dictionary definitions; urban greenery is good for well-being too. A number of unique British gardens challenge the concept of what a typical garden is. Charles Jencks' Garden of Cosmic Speculation in Dumfries and Galloway is a beautiful 30-acre (12Ha) landscaped garden on a grand scale, based on the metaphor of waves. The structures and layout reflect themes from biology, cosmology, mathematics and physics and philosophy.[10] It contains some parts which look more like the traditional enclosed garden plots (the DNA garden), but it is too large to have clearly visible boundaries. The artist and performer Derek Jarman actively rejected the concept of the garden as an enclosed retreat in his Dungeness shingle garden near the sea. It is a site open to its surroundings, reflecting Jarman's campaigning on HIV and AIDS. And Ian Finlay Hamilton's garden, Little Sparta (near Edinburgh), disrupts the idea of peaceful garden visiting by using challenging installations and objects reminiscent of warfare.

Sustainable gardening and permaculture, an extreme version of recycling, may not always look like conventional suburban gardening either, but they have the same positive beneficial capacities. In the context of industrialised agriculture, relying on the use of chemicals, permaculture can be seen as another form of political action through a commitment to sustainability, and is a demonstration of environmental identity. Mike Feingold, a permaculture practitioner in Bristol, considers that permaculture is revolution dressed up as gardening.[11] The ethical principles of permaculture are about recycling all resources in the service of caring for people and the earth. What started as *permanent agriculture* has become *permanent culture* and suggests that everyone could be self-sufficient from their own back gardens and allotments through a process of sustainable and efficient cultivation and recycling. Permaculture and environmentally sustainable practices could be thought of as another means of blurring the boundaries between self and nature, and between gardening and agriculture.

BEING OR BECOMING GARDENER IN THE 21ST CENTURY

Most everyday gardening is done by people who like to garden, either as casual weekend gardeners or as serious and keen gardeners. Gardeners say there is always something new to learn, from nature as well as from experts. But being any sort of gardener can involve learning from books, learning by doing – signing up for courses or serving an apprenticeship – or sharing information and expertise with others. Membership in gardening organisations such as the American Community Garden Association or the British Hardy Plant Society expresses personal interest and gardening identity. Garden visiting is an opportunity to pick up new ideas, and there is no shortage of available advice from experts on how to garden.

There are still plenty of print resources – handbooks, plant directories, instruction manuals – that provide advice about all sorts of gardening. There are annual gardening publications, books and monthly magazines providing advice and garden-related books for gardeners of all levels of interest and experience. Television coverage of gardening, garden shows and garden history provides advice, information and entertainment in the viewers' living room, or on the move via their laptop. People join local gardening clubs; they can access dedicated websites for advice about plants, pests and gardening techniques, or they can use an app on their phone. The internet gives instant access to a vast range of gardening information, knowledge and advice from a variety of organisations and individuals, qualified and unqualified, as well as sources of plants, specialist nurseries and gardening equipment. Gardeners can share good ideas or disasters through blogs and email. Social media platforms, such as (currently) Facebook, Instagram, Snapchat, Twitter and Pinterest, mean that people can show off their dahlias or their tomatoes and get feedback without even having to leave their garden. In addition, people can become experts by using online or downloadable gardening programmes and applications that allow them to design and plan their own real gardens.

Gardeners interviewed often say that a particular television gardening programme or gardener prompted them to start gardening or try a particular technique. The presenters on gardening programmes become gardening celebrities in their own right. They are definitely perceived as experts and classed as real gardeners. UK BBC television garden presenters, for example, all have horticultural or gardening qualifications, as well as their own gardening experience, and are thus highly credible expert gardeners. There are celebrity women gardeners, though not as many as men, and women have made significant contributions to gardening and garden design: Gertrude Jekyll and Beth Chatto spring to mind, and Alys Fowler, Carol Klein and Esther Dean are not far behind. People often have a favourite celebrity gardener, whose style is more in tune with their own, just as they have favourite cooks or singers. Celebrity gardeners are not new, though media visibility means that they have a far greater reach than some of their predecessors.

An area of debate, arising partly from its popularity on television, has been 'instant gardening'. Instant gardening usually refers to televised garden make-over programmes and is often not popular with serious gardeners. It doesn't qualify as proper 'getting your hands dirty' gardening and does not reflect the processes of growing and engaging with nature that are the essence of gardening, though the finished result can have the same beneficial effects. However, instant gardening is what happens for any big garden or horticultural show, which sees full-size trees and structures trucked on to sites to create an 'established' garden in a few days. The difference is that shows are only temporary. One concern has been the possible impact of instant gardens on the form and method of gardening, in particular the use of hard landscaping, which removes greenery and can limit space for nature, especially butterflies, and potentially for gardening. It links with the findings from Australia that householders are extending their properties further into their gardens to create more indoor space, potentially at the expense of green space. The greener the (sub)urban space, the healthier its residents. Loss of green space reduces the availability of nearby nature for restoration and improved mood.

As residents and new buildings replace greenery with rooms and hard-standing for cars, the loss of front gardens is an additional concern in England. More space for cars means less for greenery. Loss of grass, hedges and trees in front gardens means there is less capacity to absorb water and to mitigate polluting exhaust fumes in urban and suburban areas. The RHS Greening Grey Britain project[12] recommends ways to incorporate greenery and planting within these spaces to offset the impact of hard surfaces. Vertical walls of planting, or green surfaces, can help to green the built environment and provide opportunities for micro-restoration.

By 2050, 70% of the population will live in cities. The separation of home and work represented by the suburbs is no longer a reality in a 24-hour culture – work is done in cafés or on the bus. Sustainable forms of nearby nature and green spaces for relaxation and growing food are arguably needed more than ever at the same time as being under the greatest threat. Even now, most people in cities do not visit nature. If more young people want to garden, the pressure for space to garden will increase. Single people without children are satisfied if their residence has a balcony, and it is possible to do fantastic container gardening on a balcony. Alternatively, shared or community gardening may be an option. Traditionally, the options for people who have limited home space for gardening have been allotments, but these are in short supply. There are long waiting lists for allotments in large cities, and local authorities are charged to make more space available as part of social prescribing for health improvement. Allotment organisations have split plots to meet demand, or local residents join together to share larger plots that they work collectively. Pop-up gardens or pocket parks, created by large containers on the street, are one way to have access to space for gardening (see Figure 6.1) and

Figure 6.1 A pop-up garden in the middle of a busy road junction

Note: One of the residents living on the road has claimed what was a derelict municipal flower bed, cleared it and created an ornamental garden. The local council were persuaded to provide a water source, so that the garden could flourish. It provides a talking point for drivers stopped at the traffic lights.

to green the environment, although they require council permissions and commitment from the community to keep them functioning.

There is guerrilla gardening to fall back on, or taking plants to work, where there may be gardening clubs or projects. Plants in the office, as in hospitals, have a positive effect on stress and are relaxing. On the back of computer-game technology, immersive virtual reality and simulations offer people the possibility of virtual gardens in their homes or workplaces on a permanent or temporary basis. Versions of this type of immersive experience and virtual worlds are already being tried with older people and with dementia sufferers, who found seeing images through immersive technology relaxing and enjoyable.[13] Live streaming from real gardens and 360° photography mean the possibility of having beautiful gardens even in a small apartment is pretty high. It might be possible to have virtual garden shows. Research supports the benefits of virtual gardens in principle, since images of nature and views are already effective at restoring mental fatigue (Chapter 3). One of the reasons that people give up or dislike gardening is that there are too many chores, too much commitment; it's too demanding. By comparison, nature away from the home or domestic garden is there whenever it is needed for a bike ride or a walk and makes no demands. Virtual gardening could make gardeners of everyone, and they could have a starring role in their own garden show. Whether gardeners currently working on their gardens would consider virtual gardening a reasonable alternative to spending the day outside on their plot is an open question.

GARDENING AS OCCUPATION

Gardening has been described as work and as an occupation. Horticultural therapy is a form of occupational therapy, and occupational therapy is about finding ways to occupy people, through work, through crafts and through gardening. The idea of an occupation, a role that defines identity, familiar from discussion of the gardening career and the gardening identity, refers to an occupation in the sense of a job. But occupation has other meanings; occupation conveys a taking over of territory, so as well as having an occupation, you can occupy a seat or a garden or a derelict space. Thus, gardening is a form of occupation of the garden. As a gardener, you are occupied by the garden, your duties are defined, it takes up your time and keeps you busy. It also 'invades' you and becomes who you are.

There are several modes of occupation.[14] They offer an alternative way to consider the themes of identity and the human–nature relationship that have been addressed in the context of gardening and what gardeners themselves say. The *naturalistic* mode refers to us occupying the garden as an enclosed and almost spiritual place for everyday wonder, looking out to nature, and contrasting the garden with elsewhere, busy clock time with nature's time. The naturalistic mode reflects the sensations and perceptions of 'being in the garden' and the feeling of engagement with nature. In *nostalgic* mode, the garden occupies us, embodied in us through memories, reflections and feelings. This mode is about a sense of absence rather than presence; the garden occupies us as a place where recollections of relationships and people can be located in their absence, either because they have gone or we have moved on, from childhood, for example. A *pragmatic* mode of occupation is about occupation in the sense of a job (described earlier), which involves the working on and working at creating the garden, as well as a personal story, together with gardening skills and knowledge. The fourth mode of occupation – *mimetic* – is like the nostalgic mode; it is about social interaction in the garden in the present and the garden as an arena for relationships with other people in real time as well as in memories.

These modes of occupation reflect the ways that people talk about their gardening experience in research that gave rise to the themes addressed in this book. In thinking of gardening as a combination of person, process and place, the concept of occupation expresses the internal and external aspect of the psychological experience.

CONCLUDING REMARKS: 'I LOVE GARDENING. IT'S JUST A WAY OF LIFE'

The variety of different psychological concepts that has been explored in relation to gardening make it clear that there is no single psychology of gardening. The topics here have been considered under an umbrella of environmental psychology, which started from a position that people affect and are affected by their environment and by nature, that the person and the environment are always in the process of interacting in some way. Gardening is a very clear demonstration of this constant inter-connection between person, process and place. As a consequence, gardening, a commonplace activity undertaken frequently but not exclusively by older people, deserves attention by psychology.

If you enjoy it, gardening can provide a lifetime of pleasure; it's about being yourself, in a place that you created, engaging with a physical process of continuous change.

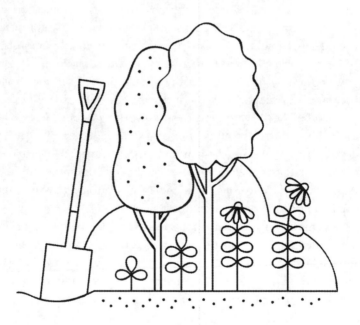

FURTHER RESOURCES

If you are intrigued by why gardens matter and mean so much to people, then you might like *A Philosophy of Gardens* by David E. Cooper (Oxford UP, 2006).

For a thorough discussion of allotment gardening, *The Allotment: Its Landscape and Culture* by David Crouch and Colin Ward (Fives Leaves Books, 1997) is now a classic, filled with anecdotes and local detail.

If you are interested in reading more about the psychology of time, Claudia Hammond's book *Time Warped: Unlocking the Mystery of Time Perception* (Canongate, 2013) is a highly readable book about the complexities of how we perceive time, by a science broadcaster who is also a psychologist.

Other people's gardens are always of interest. Penelope Lively's latest book, *Life in the Garden* (Fig Tree, 2017), is both a personal memoir of her own gardens and an exploration of gardens in literature.

Dan O'Brien's edited collection *Gardening: Philosophy for Everyone* (Wiley-Blackwell, 2010) is a really interesting gathering of ideas on all aspects of gardening and the meaning of gardens.

If you like a book with a few more pictures, then two works edited by Annette Giesecke and Naomi Jacobs address many topics covered here, and lots of others: *Earth Perfect? Nature, Utopia and the Garden* (Black Dog Publishing, 2012) and *The Good Gardener? Nature, Humanity and the Garden* (Artifice, 2015).

FICTION REFERRING TO GARDENS, GARDENERS, GARDENING OR PLANTS

The book *Elizabeth and Her German Garden* by Elizabeth von Arnim (originally published in 1898) is definitely worth a try. Elizabeth is a devoted and enthusiastic gardener whose diary has joyous descriptions of plants. Modern readers may find some of her views difficult to take.

Another noteworthy book is Penelope Lively, *The Revenge of Samuel Stokes* (1992, Puffin Books, children's fiction). Here, the ghost of a landscape gardener seeking revenge upsets the residents of a new housing estate.

Another children's story involving gardens, and the concept of time, is *Tom's Midnight Garden* by Philippa Pearce (originally published by Oxford UP, 1958). It has been made into BBC TV series and a film (1999 directed by Willard Carroll).

For a story set on an allotment site, you could try *The Mulberry Tree* by George Mournehis, (2014).

SUGGESTED FILMS THAT SPECIFICALLY FEATURE DIFFERENT FACETS OF GARDENS, GARDENERS OR GARDENING

Being There (Hal Ashby, 1979). Peter Sellers plays a gardener whose identity as a gardener is central to his sense of who he is and what he does. His gardening statements are interpreted as words of wisdom by businesses and politicians, and he becomes US president.

The Day of the Triffids (Steve Sekely, 1962). This classic horror-cum-sci-fi film based on John Wyndham's novel is a post-apocalyptic vision of carnivorous plants able to move and communicate that puts worrying about the weeding in the shade.

The Draughtsman's Contract (Peter Greenaway, 1982). This is a puzzling 17th-century murder mystery involving landscape designers and gardeners as key characters and incorporates the idea of nature as an actor into the story.

Greenfingers (Hal Ashby, 2000). Loosely based on a true story, this is story of prison inmates who took to gardening and ended up winning prizes at a prestigious national flower show, emphasising both the restorative and the social benefits of gardening.

WEBSITES

If therapeutic horticulture appeals, then visit the Thrive website. Their motto is 'using gardening to change lives':
www.thrive.org.uk

For an inspiring call to action to garden outside traditional home gardening, try this site:
www.ted.com/talks/ron_finley_a_guerilla_gardener_in_south_central_la

The original English guerrilla gardener's blog is a useful way of finding out more about what can be achieved as a guerrilla gardener:
www.guerrillagardening.org

For an entertaining view of how to match your garden to your personality have a look at this website, but take it with a pinch of salt:
www.houzz.com/ideabooks/20363980/list/what-kind-of-gardener-are-you-find-your-archetype

To get an idea of how marketers see gardeners, you can download details of the different profiles of gardening consumers from the Horticultural Trades Association website:
https://hta.org.uk/learn-develop/market-information/consumer-segmentation.html

NOTES

CHAPTER 1

1 Hall, T. (2010). Where have all the gardens gone? *Australian Planner*, 45, 30–37.

2 Statista, The Statistics Portal, www.statista.com/statistics/227419/number-of-gardeners-usa/

3 Cavanagh, S.T. cited in Thorpe, C. (2016). Great literary gardens from Hamlet to Lady Chatterley's lover. *Financial Times*, 16 May 2016. Retrieved 22 April 2017 from www.ft.com/content/2c2d36ce-0e06-11e6-b41f-0beb7e589515?mhq5j=e3

4 Kaplan, R. (1973). Some psychological benefits of gardening. *Environment & Behavior*, 5, 145–152.

5 Freeman, C., Dickinson, K.J.M., Porter, S., & van Heezik, Y. (2012). 'My garden is an expression of me': Exploring householders' relationships with their gardens. *Journal of Environmental Psychology*, 32, 135–143 (p. 135).

6 Herzog, T.R., Maguire, C.P., & Nebel, M.B. (2003). Assessing the restorative components of environments. *Journal of Environmental Psychology*, 23, 150–170.

7 Mayer, F. S., & Frantz, C. M. (2004). The connectedness to nature scale: A measure of individuals' feeling in community with nature. *Journal of Environmental Psychology*, 24, 503–515.

8 Clayton, S. (2003). Environmental identity: A conceptual and an operational definition. In S. Clayton & S. Opotow (Eds.), *Identity and the natural environment: The psychological significance of nature* (pp. 45–65). Cambridge, MA: MIT Press.

9 Clayton, S. (2007). Domesticated nature: Motivations for gardening and perceptions of environmental impact. *Journal of Environmental Psychology, 27,* 215–244.

10 Cervinka, R., Schwab, M., Schonbauer, R., Hammerle, I., Pirgie, L., & Sudkamp, J. (2016). My garden – my mate? Perceived restorativeness of private gardens and its predictors. *Urban Forestry & Urban Greening, 16,* 182–187.

11 Bhatti, M. (2006). When I'm in the garden I can create my own Paradise: Homes and gardens in later life. *Sociological Review, 54,* 318–341.

12 The Mass Observation Archive, University of Sussex, www.massobs.org.uk

13 Corker, K.S., Donellan, M.B., Kim, S.Y., Schwartz, S.J., & Zamboanga, B.L. (2017). College student samples are not always equivalent: The magnitude of personality differences across colleges and universities. *Journal of Personality, 85,* 123–135.

CHAPTER 2

1 Use of quotations: Quotes without names attached are from interviews with gardeners who consented to take part in our research projects. In a few cases, quotes are attributed to named individuals. With one exception, these are not their real names. Special thanks to all the gardeners for their time and contribution to this book. All other direct quotes are attributed and sources listed.

2 Kerr, W. (2015, September 19). How does your garden grow. *Guardian Weekend,* p. 95.

3 Li, W.W., Hodgetts, D., & Ho, E. (2012). Gardens, transitions and identity reconstruction among older Chinese immigrants to New Zealand. *Journal of Health Psychology, 15,* 67–86.

4 Freeman, C., Dickinson, K.J.M., Porter, S., & van Heezik, Y. (2012). 'My garden is an expression of me': Exploring householders' relationships with their gardens. *Journal of Environmental Psychology, 32,* 135–143.

5 Van den Berg, A.E., & van Winsum-Westra, M. (2010). Manicured, romantic or wild? The relation between need for structure and preferences for garden styles. *Urban Forestry & Urban Greening, 9,* 179–186.

6 Dunnett, N., & Qasim, M. (2000). Perceived benefit to human well-being of urban gardens. *Horttechnology, 10,* 40–45.

7 Rhodes, R.E., & Smith, N.E.I. (2012). Personality correlates of physical activity: A review and meta-analysis. *British Journal of Sports Medicine, 40,* 958–965.

8 Donellan, M.B., & Lucas, R.E. (2008). Age differences in the Big Five across the lifespan: Evidence from two national samples. *Psychology of Aging*, 53, 558–566.

9 Jaspal, R., & Breakwell, G. (Eds.). (2014). *Identity process theory: Identity, social action and social change*. Cambridge, UK: Cambridge UP.

10 Tajfel, H. (1982). Social psychology of intergroup relations. *Annual Review of Psychology*, 33, 1–39.

11 Stebbins, R. (2007). *Serious leisure: A perspective for our time*. New Brunswick, NJ: Transaction Publishers.

12 Bhatti, M., Church, A., Claremont, A., & Stenner, P. (2009). I love being in the garden: Enchanting encounters in everyday life. *Social and Cultural Geography*, 10, 61–76 (p. 69).

13 Raisborough, J., & Bhatti, M. (2007). Women's leisure and auto/biography: Empowerment and resistance in the garden. *Journal of Leisure Research*, 39, 459–476.

14 Proshansky, H.M., Fabian, A.K., & Kaminoff, R. (1983). Place-identity: Physical world socialization of the self. *Journal of Environmental Psychology*, 3, 57–83 (p. 60).

15 Manzo, L.C., & Devine-Wright, P. (Eds.). (2014) *Place attachment: Advances in theory, methods and applications*. Abingdon, Oxon: Routledge.

16 Scannell, L., & Gifford, R. (2017). Place attachment enhances psychological need satisfaction. *Environment & Behavior*, 49, 1–31.

17 Heidegger, M. (1993). Building dwelling thinking. In M. Heidegger, *Basic writings* (Rev. ed., pp. 343–364). London: Routledge.

18 Bachelard, G. (1958/1994). *The poetics of space*. Boston, MA: Beacon Publishers.

19 Wardhaugh, J. (1999). The unaccommodated woman: Home, homelessness and identity. *Sociological Review*, 47, 92–109.

CHAPTER 3

1 Kaplan, R., & Kaplan, S. (1989). *The experience of nature*. Cambridge, MA: Cambridge University Press.

2 Csikszentmihalyi, M. (1975/2000). *Beyond boredom and anxiety* (25th anniversary ed.). San Francisco: Jossey-Bass.

3 Brown, K.W., & Ryan, R.M. (2003). The benefits of being present: Mindfulness and its role in psychological wellbeing. *Journal of Personality and Social Psychology*, 84, 822–848.

4   Droit-Volet, S., & Meck, W. (2008). How emotions colour our perceptions of time. *Trends in Cognitive Science*, 11, 504–513.

5   Ulrich, R.S. (1983). Aesthetic and affective response to natural environment. In I. Altman & J.F. Wohlwill (Eds.), *Human behaviour and environment: Advances in theory and research* (Vol. 6, pp. 85–125). New York: Plenum Press.

6   Kaplan, R., & Kaplan, S. (1989). *The experience of nature*. Cambridge, MA: Cambridge University Press.

7   Cervinka, R., Schwab, M., Schonbauer, R., Hammerle, I., Pirgie, L., & Sudkamp, J. (2016). My garden – my mate? Perceived restorativeness of private gardens and its predictors. *Urban Forestry & Urban Greening*, 15, 182–187.

8   Kaplan, R. (2001) The nature of the view from home. *Environment & Behavior*, 33, 507–542.

9   Lee, K.E., Williams, K.J.H., Sargent, L.D., Williams, N.S.G., & Johnson, K.A. (2015). 40-second green roof views sustain attention: The role of microbreaks in attention restoration. *Journal of Environmental Psychology*, 42, 182–189.

10 Ratcliffe, E., Gatersleben, B., & Sowden, T. (2016). Associations with bird sounds: How do they relate to perceived restorative potential? *Journal of Environmental Psychology*, 47, 136–144.

11 Scopelliti, M., & Giuliani, M.V. (2004). Choosing restorative environments across the lifespan: A matter of place experience. *Journal of Environmental Psychology*, 24, 423–437.

12 Morton, T.A., van der Bles, A.M., & Haslam, S.A., (2017). Seeing our self reflected in the world around us: the role of identity in making (natural) environments restorative. *Journal of Environmental Psychology*, 49, 65–77.

13 Csikszentmihalyi, M. (1975/2000). *Beyond boredom and anxiety* (25th anniversary ed.). San Francisco: Jossey-Bass (p. 43).

14 Anderson, N.D., Lau, M.A., Segal, Z.V., & Bishop, S.R. (2007). Mindfulness-based stress reduction and attentional control. *Clinical Psychology & Psychotherapy*, 14, 449–463.

15 Lymeus, F., Lundgren, T., & Hartig, T. (2017). Attentional effort of beginning mindfulness training is offset with practice directed to images of natural scenery. *Environment & Behavior*, 49, 536–559.

16 Schutte, N.S., & Malouf, J.M. (2011). Emotional intelligence mediates the relationship between mindfulness and subjective wellbeing. *Personality & Individual Differences*, 50, 1116–1119.

17 Howell, A.J., Dopko, R.J., Passmore, H., & Buro, K. (2011). Nature connectedness: Associations with well-being and mindfulness. *Personality and Individual Differences*, 51, 166–171.

18 Tang, Y., Holzel, B. K., & Posner, M. I. (2015). The neuroscience of mindfulness meditation. *Nature Reviews Neuroscience*, 16, 213–225.

CHAPTER 4

1 Kellert, S. R., & Wilson, E. O. (Eds.). (1993). *The biophilia hypothesis*. Washington, DC: Island Press.

2 Gatersleben, B., & Andrews, M. (2013). When walking in nature is not restorative – the role of prospect and refuge. *Health & Place*, 20, 91–101.

3 Appleton, J. (1975). *The experience of landscape*. New York: Wiley.

4 Wolfgang Buttress, Hive sculpture details, www.wolfgangbuttress.com/expo-2015/

5 Hagerhall, C. M., Purcell, T., & Taylor, R. P. (2004). Fractal dimension of landscape silhouette as a predictor of landscape preference. *Journal of Environmental Psychology*, 24, 247–255.

6 Joye, Y. (2007). Architectural lessons from environment psychology: The case of biophilic architecture. *Review of General Psychology*, 11, 305–328.

7 Lindal, P. J., & Hartig, T. (2013). Architectural variation, building height, and the restorative quality of urban residential streetscapes. *Journal of Environmental Psychology*, 33, 26–36.

8 Gibson, J. J. (1979). *The ecological approach to visual perception*. Boston: Houghton Mifflin.

9 Falk, J. H., & Balling, J. D. (2010). Evolutionary influence on human landscape preference. *Environment & Behaviour*, 42, 479–493.

10 Hartmann, P., & Apaolaza-Ibanez, V. (2010). Beyond savanna: An evolutionary and environmental psychology approach to behavioral effects of nature scenery in green advertising. *Journal of Environmental Psychology*, 30, 119–128.

11 Baker, B. (2004). *Why we garden: Stories of a British obsession*. London: Aston House Press, p. 95.

12 Lively, P. (2013, October 5). So this is old age. *Guardian Saturday Review*, pp. 2–4.

13 Power, E. (2005). Human-nature relations in suburban gardens. *Australian Geographer*, 36, 39–53.

14 Love, A. (2016, November 19). How does your garden grow. *Guardian Weekend*, p. 110.

15 Latour, B. (2005). *Reassembling the social: An introduction to actor-network-theory*. Oxford: Oxford UP.

16 Hitchings, R. (2003). People, plants and performance: On actor-network theory and the material pleasures of the private garden. *Social & Cultural Geography*, 4, 99–113.

17 Francis, M., & Hester, R.T. (Eds.). (1990). *The meaning of gardens*. Cambridge, MA: MIT Press, p. 94.

18 Bixler, R.D., & Floyd, M.F. (1997). Nature is scary, disgusting and uncomfortable. *Environment & Behavior*, 29, 443–467.

19 Koole, S.L., & van den Berg, A.E. (2005). Lost in the wilderness: Terror management action orientation, and nature evaluation. *Journal of Personality & Social Psychology*, 88, 1014–1028.

20 Van Andel, J. (1990). Places children like, dislike and fear. *Children's Environment Quarterly*, 7, 24–31.

21 Lin, B.B., Gaston, K.J., Fuller, R.A., Wu, D., Bush, R., & Shanahan, D.F. (2017). How green is your garden? Urban form and sociodemographic factors influence yard vegetation, visitation, and ecosystem service benefits. *Landscape & Urban Planning*, 157, 239–246.

22 Lumber, R., Richardson, M., & Sheffield, D. (2017). Beyond knowing nature: Contact, emotion, compassion, meaning, and beauty are pathways to nature connection. *PLoS One*, doi:10.1371/journal.pone.0177186. Retrieved 4 November 2017.

CHAPTER 5

1 Unruh, A.M. (2004). The meaning of gardens and gardening in daily life: Comparison between gardeners and non-gardeners. *Acta Horticulture*, 639, 67–72 (p. 69).

2 Buck, D. (2016). *Gardens for health: Implications for policy and practice*. London: Kings Fund Report.

3 van den Berg, A.E., van Winsum-Westra, M., de Vries, S., & van Dillen, S.M.E. (2010). Allotment gardening & health: A comparative survey among allotment gardeners & their neighbors without an allotment. *Environmental Health*, 9, 74.

4 Wood, C.J., Pretty, J., & Griffin, M. (2016). A case control study of the health and wellbeing benefits of allotment gardening. *Journal of Public Health*, 38, e336–e344.

5 Soga, M., Cox, D.T.C., Yamaura, Y., Gaston, K.J., Kurisi, K., & Hanaki, K. (2017). Health benefits of urban allotment gardening: Improved physical and psychological wellbeing and social integration. *International Journal of Environmental Research & Public Health*, 14, 71.

6 Webber, J., Hinds, J., & Camic, P.M. (2015). The wellbeing of allotment gardeners: A mixed methodological study. *Ecopsychology*, 7, 20–28.

7   van den Berg, A.E., & Custers, M.H.G. (2011). Gardening promotes neuro-endocrine and affective restoration from stress. *Journal of Health Psychology*, 16, 3–11.

8   Orr, N., Wagstaffe, A., Briscoe, S., & Garside, R. (2016). How do older people describe their sensory experiences of the natural world? A systematic review. *BMC Geriatrics*, 16, 116.

9   Carstensen, L.L. (2006). The influence of a sense of time on human development. *Science*, 312, 1913–1915.

10 Cipriani, J., Benz, A., Holmgren, A., Kinter, D., McGarry, J., & Rufino, G. (2017). A systematic review of the effects of horticultural therapy on persons with mental health conditions. *Occupational Therapy in Mental Health*, 33, 47–69.

11 Bishop, R., & Purcell, E. (2006). The value of an allotment group for refugees. *British Journal Occupational Therapy*, 76, 264–269.

12 Whear, R., Thompson Coon, J., Bethel, A., Abbott, R., Stein, K., & Garside, R. (2014). What is the impact of using outdoor spaces such as gardens on the wellbeing of those with dementia. *Journal of the American Directors Association*, 15, 697–705.

13 Sempik, J., Aldridge, J., & Becker, S. (2005). *Health, wellbeing and social inclusion*. Bristol: Policy Press.

14 Kohlkeppel, T., Bradley, J.C., & Jacob, S. (2002). A walk through the garden: Can a visit to a botanic garden reduce stress. *Horttechnology*, 12, 489–492.

15 Firth C., May, D., & Pearson, D. (2011). Developing 'community' in community gardens. *Local Environment*, 16, 555–568.

16 Draper, C., & Freedman, D. (2010). Review and analysis of the benefits, purposes and motivations associated with community gardens in the US. *Journal of Community Practice*, 18, 458–492.

17 Ulrich, R.S. (1984). View from a window may influence recovery from surgery. *Science*, 224, 420–422.

18 Park, S.H. (2006). *Randomized clinical trials evaluating therapeutic influences of ornamental indoor plants in hospital rooms on health outcomes of patients recovering from surgery*. Unpublished Dissertation, Kansas State University, Manhattan, Kansas. Retrieved 14 March 2017 from http://hdl.handle.net/2097/227

19 Berman, M.G., Kross, E., Krpan, K.M., Askren, M.K., Burson. A., Deldin, P.J., . . . Jonides, J. (2012). Interacting with nature improves cognition and affect for individuals with depression. *Journal of Affective Disorders*, 140, 300–305.

20 Thompson Coon, J., Boddy, K., Stein, K., Whear, R., Barton, S., & Depledge, M.H. (2011). Does participating in physical activity in outdoor nature environments have a greater effect on physical and mental wellbeing than

physical activity indoors? A systematic review. *Environmental Science & Technology*, 45, 1761–1772.

21 Mitchell, R. (2013). Is physical activity in natural environments better for mental health than activity in other environments? *Social Science & Medicine*, 91, 130–134.

22 Duvall, J. (2011). Enhancing the benefits of outdoor walking with cognitive engagement strategies. *Journal of Environmental Psychology*, 31, 27–35.

23 Kardan, O., Gozdyra, P., Misic, N., Moola, F., Palmer, L. J., Puas, T., & Berman, M. G. (2015). Neighbourhood greenspace and health in a large urban centre. *Nature Scientific Reports*, 5, 11610. Retrieved 21 May 2017 from www.nature.com/scientificreports/

24 De Young, R., Scheuer, K., Brown, T., Crow, T., & Stewart, J. (2017). Some psychological benefits of urban nature: Mental vitality from time spent in nearby nature. In A. M. Columbus (Ed.), *Advances in Psychology Research* (Vol. 116, pp. 94–120). New York: Nova Science.

25 De Vries, S. (2010). Nearby nature and human health: Looking at the mechanisms and their implications. In C. Ward Thompson, P. Aspinall, & S. Bell (Eds.), *Open space: People space 2, innovative approaches to researching landscape and health* (pp. 75–94). Abingdon: Routledge.

26 Ryan, R. M., & Deci, E. L. (2001). On happiness and human potentials: A review of research on hedonic and eudaimonic well-being. *Annual Review of Psychology*, 52, 141–166.

27 Capaldi, C., Dopko, R. L., & Zelenski, J. (2014). The relationship between nature connectedness and happiness: A meta-analysis. *Frontiers in Psychology*, 5, 976.

CHAPTER 6

1 Raisborough, J., & Bhatti, M. (2007). Women's leisure and auto/biography: Empowerment and resistance in the garden. *Journal of Leisure Research*, 39, 459–476.

2 Parker, R. (2005). Unnatural history. In T. Richardson & N. Kingsbury (Eds.), *Vista: The culture and politics of gardens* (pp. 87–99). London: Frances Lincoln.

3 Parry, D. C., Glover, T. D., & Shinew, K. J. (2005). 'Mary Mary quite contrary, how does your garden grow?' Examining gender roles and relations in community gardens. *Leisure Studies*, 24, 177–192.

4 Calogiuri, G. (2016). Natural environments & childhood experiences: Promoting physical activity, examining the meditational effects of feeling about nature and social networks. *International Journal of Environment & Public Health*, 13, 439.

5   Scott, T.L., Masser, B.M., & Pachana, N.A. (2015). Exploring the health and wellbeing benefits of gardening for older adults. *Ageing & Society*, 35, 2176–2200.

6   Wiseman, T. (2012). Gardens: Opportunities and threats from an occupational perspective. College of Occupational Therapists Annual Conference, SECC Glasgow, Scotland, 12–14 June.

7   Thompson, M. (2015). Between boundaries: From commoning and guerrilla gardening to community and trust development in Liverpool. *Antipode*, 47, 1021–1042.

8   McKay, G. (2011). *Radical gardens: Politics, idealism and rebellion in the garden*. London: Frances Lincoln.

9   The Pansy Project, www.thepansyproject.com

10 Garden of Cosmic Speculation, www.charlesjencks.com/#!the-garden-of-cosmic-speculation or www.scotlandsgardens.org/gardens/garden/6f8a52d7-f7b0-45c2-91fc-999e00d2ac95

11 See for example https://growingarden.wordpress.com/

12 Royal Horticultural Society (n.d.). *Greening Grey Britain*. Retrieved 2 November 2017 from www.rhs.org.uk/science/gardening-in-a-changing-world/greening-grey-britain

13 Ang, C.S. (n.d.). Retrieved 9 June 2017 from www.irishnews.com/magazine/science/2017/05/15/news/watch-how-virtual-reality-is-helping-the-lives-of-dementia-patients-1026839/

14 Stenner, P., Church, A., & Bhatti, M. (2012). Human landscape relations and the occupation of space: Experiencing and expressing domestic gardens. *Environment & Planning A*, 44, 1712–1727.